Dare to Doubt

Further conversations between GOD

and

BETTY GREEN

DARE TO DOUBT

Printed by The Leiston Press, Suffolk

Published by VISION unlimited
Belvedere
Brodick
Isle of Arran
KA27 8AZ

To obtain further copies of this book
please telephone 0845 644 8623
or e-mail daretodoubt@vision-unlimited.co.uk

ISBN: 0-9545514-4-3

Also by Betty Green:

Good God
a surprising dialogue between God and a mere mortal

Dedicated to all who wish to open their higher **mind**

be kind to their **body**

and connect with their **spirit**

Praise for Betty Green...

"Your books are written in a style that can 'touch' someone who is completely new to spirituality – as well as the long-term seeker! They speak with a loving timeless wisdom that penetrates logic – it is beautiful – one cannot help but say 'wow' after each 'answer'."

James Eckhardt

"Because Love is the golden thread running through this wonderful book, I feel it is a vital antidote to the world's news of hate and fear which bombards our consciousness daily. As a child who was brought up on the 'fear' of God, a book like this has turned my beliefs upside down – rather the right way up!. I hope and pray this amazing, comforting and thrilling book will get to a world-wide readership and that it will engender an 'outbreak of peace and love' to help heal a wounded world."

Jennifer Toombes

"...answers all my specific spiritual queries."

Edna Fisher

CONTENTS

March 2004

So my sabbatical is over. It has been more than a year since I tuned-in to God.

It hasn't been a wasted year. I have achieved quite a lot; I have learned a lot from further reading; I have experienced a lot from other people's attitudes.

It was interesting to experience the ins and outs of printing and publishing a book. I was led to the most helpful, charming firm of printers – a family business willing to advise me at every turn. But I am glad I am not writing for a living!

I cannot use the Big Boys to stock or distribute copies of "Good God" because they demand such a very high mark-up. I would lose on every copy. The independent book shops are willing to accept a low mark-up because they take copies on Sale or Return. I personally deliver the books all over East Anglia, by car, then on foot, as postage would usually cost more than petrol. I have also discovered it is cheaper to post three books as one plus two, even allowing for the cost of the special bags!

The most enlightening discovery of all is that calling on Bible Shops and Christian Book Shops with my seemingly very Christian book is a complete waste of time! Either the books are refused immediately, or on a second visit I find they have been put on one side. The reason? They are not orthodox enough.

How sad this is. It just proves that some people have set ideas about their beliefs and do not want to try to enlarge or alter their concepts. And, in the case of religious booksellers, they wish to censor what their customers shall read. Twice I was brought passages from the bible to read, just to show me that I was misguided. Conversely, I received a wonderful e-mail from a reader quoting much from Leviticus, asking me was it all right to sell his daughter into slavery, kill his neighbour for working on the Sabbath and stone his uncle for swearing. And as he shouldn't touch the skin of a dead pig, was it all right to play football if he wore gloves!

People do not appear to wish to think deeply about Life. In spite of all the horror and turmoil that is going on all over the world I suppose they feel helpless to help. If only they would understand how powerful Thought is.

I speak my thoughts to so few people. Just a very few friends are as enthralled as I am on how much we can learn. It takes a very open mind and a need to sort out the wheat from the chaff. I keep abreast with reading Neale Donald Walsch's books. It was he who inspired me to write in the first place. His latter books seem quite indigestible at first reading. Very deep. I need to concentrate and re-read many sentences. Then suddenly I wonder why I didn't absorb their simplicity.

I read to my blind friend once a week and we have just been enjoying Anthony Borg's book, "Life in the World Unseen". Her family cannot understand our interest in these things. We have decided they now think of us as "poor old dears who are getting a bit cranky". We can see the funny side of this. We may be old, but we know where we are going and what a shock it will be for them when they find out we were not off our trolleys!

I now think I am being nudged to start tuning-in again. I wonder what I am going to be told? I have a feeling it will be just a little less simple than "Good God". I do not feel full of questions this time. Those were answered as I asked them and others have been answered in Neale's books.

Please remember what I wrote before – I am no different from you. We are all One. God is not a person, but the Great Intelligence of which we are all part – there to contact. He, It, is all Love, all Understanding, all Power, all Knowing. Let us Experience IT.

Never Alone

Dear God, I wonder I am not apprehensive about talking to you after this long gap, but I have absolutely no doubt that you will again use me. What do you wish me to write about?

Hello my child, of course I am here for I never leave you, nor have I done during the last year. You cannot be apart from me and you know that.

The pink rosebud you picture has changed to a gold rose with brilliant red tips – an emblem of the sunrise. A new day is dawning. Not just a day, a new Era. Be confident. The dark clouds are passing away.

You are not yet conscious of this because there is so much turmoil, so much fighting, so much killing. And all in MY Name.

If only my children would realise that you can reach me in your own ways. It does not matter how you reach me, how you 'touch' me. I have said before it does not matter what you wear, what you do, what symbols you use, what phrases you speak.

It is what is in your hearts that matters. It is so much more simple to just BE, knowing you are my children. You do not alter your voice, your dress, your stance, to speak to your earthly parents. You know they are there and you just speak to them. They are listening to your words and looking into your eyes; they are not watching your movements or your clothing.

Life is simple. I am simple. Yes, simple. No trimmings are necessary to speak to me, to feel me within you.

You, child, have been reading how there are no boundaries on the next plane. All are welcome in each others houses and gardens. All is peace.

Why are you all rushing about? Speed causes accidents. There is No Time. Life is Eternal. Yes, Eternal. You will never die. You just move to another plane, a different vibration.

On each plane Life is what you make it. You can progress or you can stand still. Sometimes it is good to stand still and look at all the wonders about you, be they great buildings, beautiful views, calm waters, animals playing. Do you stop to think? You learn that way.

Do you care about others? Do they care about you? Are you kind, generous with your thoughts, your time?

3

Do you cheat, do you shout, do you bully, swear, rave. Does it make you feel better? If so, it is because you are using your puny power over someone else. Looking on, you don't look very admirable. Not a person to make a friend of. Not a person to admire.

Why do you want more, more, more? Are you dissatisfied with your lot? Would you rather be that sick person who cannot move without pain, cannot see clearly, has no home, no food, no clothes?

Count your blessings. Huh, you think, I don't have any. No? Look again, think again, compare again. Is there hate in your heart? Are you envious? Would you like to change places with someone else? I wonder if you would if you really knew that person. What troubles, heartaches, sorrows are they hiding?

Why not try changing your thoughts. How you feel, how you think, is up to you. You can have perfect peace. We will follow this theme, because you do not believe this at this moment in time.

Of course, if you would rather continue as you are; if you have no wish to progress, just put down this book.

Don't throw it out. You may wish to refer to it later.

Taking Responsibility

Can we, as individuals, have any effect on the killing and maiming of human beings in Iraq, Israel, Zimbabwe, to mention but a few of the countries at war?

You are all having an effect Now. You are either condoning it, indifferent to it or horrified by it. And this does not mean just you as onlookers. Think of the power of the hate and the fear of the people in those countries.

Were you able to transport yourselves into the atmosphere above all that fighting you would be choked by the fear, the smell, the foulness of it all.

I have been telling you, through so many writers, about the POWER of thought. Why do some of you pray? Because you believe your thoughts will be picked up in some miraculous way and make your wishes come true. So how does that work when one person is praying for the exact opposite of what you are? *Please make Uncle Tom better. Please let Uncle Tom die.*

Remember about "Thy Will be done, not mine"?

There is so much you forget to remember. You forget that you are all One, all loved, all known, yes known.

In that case why do you let us get into such terrible trouble, such ghastly situations?

So it's all my fault?

Well you made us initially; you say you are always with us; we are all one; we are never alone.

Isn't there something you are forgetting? What else do I remind you about?

You have Free Will.

Then wouldn't it have been better if we hadn't had Free Will? We wouldn't have got into all these troubles. Life would have been simple.

Would it?

Yes. We would always know the right thing to do and say. We would know which way to go.

Would you?

Yes. Well, wouldn't we?

Wouldn't you want Choice?

That would be nice.

Then how would you have Choice without Free Will? To bring this down to basics – your brother would say, 'We will go for a walk. We will walk towards the East, quickly.' With no choice, you would agree. With choice you might say, 'I would rather walk towards the West, slowly.'

Without wishing to sound rude, isn't this rather a silly example?

You started this vein of thought. In fact this 'silly' analogy is informative. Apply it to other decisions. At only a few months old, you start making decisions. Shall you crawl, shall you cry for food, shall you try to sit up? When older, shall you study engineering or medicine? Would you like all this to have been pre-planned?

No, although in a way I was made to do what my parents wanted me to do!

Did you like that?

No. That was why I told my own children they should do what they wished as a career.

So you gave them Free Choice.

Yes.

Did they appreciate that?

Yes, I think so. And they have used their particular talents.

You have opened up a hive of bees here, haven't you! You know how your mind is going and I know that too. You also know, roughly, where I am going to lead you, don't you?

I suggest we stop for now. Let your thoughts settle down. They are going too fast for you to pick up.

Reality

Please explain about Thought & Prayer and War & Peace.

As more and more of you wish for Peace, see Peace, make a reality of it in your Mind, so it will become a Reality. Do not ask Me to give you peace. I have already done that. Peace is your natural state of Being. It is like asking Me for Life; you already have Life. I cannot take that away because it is eternal. You do not grasp that peace is eternal and natural. When you kill you are transferring that life on to another plane. What do you gain by a lot of dead bodies?

You disturb life; you disturb peace, but only as you see it.

The I that is in you is your Conscience, the part of you that knows what is right; it knows right from wrong. You disturb your peace with wrong-doing. You know that. You know when you ill-treat another, frighten another, hit another – you KNOW it is wrong. You know it is wrong when you take what is not yours.

Whether you are taking another's wallet, another's food or another's land, you KNOW it is wrong. In the first cases it seems a small wrong, but when it comes to fighting for another's land you see what an enormous wrong it is. You see how it affects thousands of people; your own race and another's. You have no right to what does not belong to you and that applies even to your OWN land! You do not own your place in the world – I have put you there to enjoy and nurture your 'lot'. You do not own your child, your patch of air, your patch of rain, your piece of land.

You do Choose how you shall live, how you shall behave, how you shall treat your neighbour, both near and far. You, yourselves, cannot give a piece of your land to your child, but I allow you to do that. Your free choice comes in the fact that you wish to part with something you think belongs to you.

How can you really own your garden? Is it you that causes the flowers and the vegetables to grow? Are you renting it out to Me or am I renting it out to you?

Makes you think, doesn't it?

How much more this applies to the land that seems to belong to another nation.

There is no need for you to have Rights and the wrongs are when you try to exercise the Rights you really do not have! As you are all One, all part of the Whole, how can there be divisions, boundaries, rules and regulations? If you all act and live in harmony these rights and wrongs and rules and regulations become unnecessary. That is food for thought.

When you truly love someone, you want only for their good, their happiness, their completeness. THAT IS HOW I LOVE YOU. If you put this into practice yourselves there are no problems to solve. All is for Good, all is for Peace and Harmony.

How near are you to living this way?

****

I am confused. In the past you have said there is no right and wrong, yet that is what we have been talking about. Is it wrong for us, as a nation, to go to the aid of another country where its people are being persecuted by a sadistic dictator?

How do you help that country by killing thousands of its inhabitants, maiming thousands more, bringing down its buildings, causing its hospitals to be blocked with the injured?

Do you expect those people to admire you for doing this? Do they, the vast majority, understand that you could possibly be trying to help them? Is their present life now better than it was before you intervened?

Well yes, if we have destroyed the regime that was persecuting them.

7

Are those people going to like you for now enforcing your will on them in place of their previous bully? Are you not taking away their free choice? Why do you think you know better how they wish to live?

What we hope to put in place will be better for them. They will not live in fear.

Where before they were living in fear of persecution, they are now living in fear of starvation, homelessness, poverty. Do you think you have helped? Do you think you have been an example?

No, not when you put it that way.

How else can you put it?

We were trying to help them. We were sending our own military forces to their aid, putting our own countrymen at risk of being killed and maimed.

Why have you got military forces?

To protect ourselves, our land, our right to peace.

After all the talk we have had about Peace, Prayer, Thought, do you still think it is right to use force, force of any kind?

Example is what you should be using. I know you are thinking about the tyrants of this world. But I asked before, who put them into positions of power?

When you govern by Love, Honesty, Unselfishness, there will be Peace. Yes, you are thinking, but what happens in the meantime? I tell you, a start has to start somewhere or you will continue as you have done for thousands of years. There are those you think of as clever enough to make weapons of destruction. Are there not those clever enough to devise actions of Love and Understanding.

All my people want peace and plenty. It is there NOW. You have not yet learned how to use it.

You do not waste your time when you pray. Use your power to hold all countries in the Light of Peace. It is pouring down upon all your earth plane. See it. Use it. Know it. You do already know all this. It is deep within you. I put it there. There would be no need for me to make you use it – which I do not do because of your free choice.

Oh, my unenlightened little children – have pity on yourselves. Use all that is free to you to make your lives perfect. Use the Love that I am now pouring down upon you.

Keeping On

I feel a reluctance to tune-in to you, even though I know you are my greatest Friend, my constant companion. In general, people don't want to talk about You, nor hear what You are saying. They are so full of doubt, so wrapped up in their own little lives, even concerned about what they shall wear to make an impression.

I am not being judgmental, I am sorry for them. We spend millions of pounds on education, yet exclude the most important subject of all – YOU.

I would not be asked, nor even allowed, to pass on what you are teaching me, to schools or at meetings in general, because it is considered 'religious'. Yet the true story of Life is so exciting, such a challenge, so rewarding – and with a Happy Ending, though you and I know it is not an ending.

We can learn all the time, worthwhile stuff. I had the privilege of visiting my old friend, John Kemp, yesterday. He is such a wise, old soul. He told me about some of his past incarnations and I could have listened for hours.

Are my puny efforts making any impression?

How is your rose appearing?

It is upright and remains gold, tipped with red, instead of the past pink bud.

And it is fully open. Do you recall when you were fearful of your previous rose bud becoming upright, because you felt you would not be able to cope with its message? Now it is not only upright, it is fully open and it has changed colour.

Oh dear God, that means you will not give me more than I can cope with; too much for me to be able to pass on in this form. That gives me a feeling of great humility, yet enormous joy. It gives me the push, the urge, that I needed to carry on with this, your work.

We have spoken before about raindrops becoming a lake. Neale's work is reaching millions (Neale Donald Walsch). That hasn't taken so long to reach those who are crying out for my Truth, has is? If only one in each dozen of your friends is finding this 'interesting' isn't that a pointer, an encouragement? You cannot see your first book's progress, but I tell you, you cannot stop it. If you decided it was all nonsense, it is too late now to stop its outcome.

What a challenging thought! What a responsibility! I could have been putting a lot of false ideas into the minds of readers! Of course, that is what has happened in the past, and is still happening today. Writers have put their

9

OWN ideas on to paper and wanted others to believe them as Truth. And others HAVE believed them as Truth and added to them and altered them and so we have all these different religions and warring peoples – all in the name of 'what you didn't give them'.

That is where we can sort out the wheat from the chaff as we read all the different accounts of what You really want us to know, to remember. All becomes clear when we truly 'tune-in' to you. When we get that 'direct line to God' we hear only your Truth. We have to be very sure not to add our own ideas or feelings or interpretations. May I ever be a 'Channel for Your Light'. May I never add one iota to what I 'hear'. Thank you, dear God, for giving me new ambition to carry on.

Beyond the Darkness

How will we start to see this new sunrise?

The Light is beckoning you to follow it. More and more of you are realising you cannot make progress with your present methods. You are so tired of listening to your leaders, governments, news bulletins, all talking about war and terrorism.

You have a great desire to get beyond the black clouds, the dark skies. You want to know if there is something more worthwhile on the other side; not the other side in the heaven world, but the other side of this darkness and fear. Most of you now have fears, if not for yourselves, fears for someone known to you who is 'out there', either fighting or living in a dangerous place.

You are getting disillusioned about the way your food and water is tampered with. You are learning that much of what you are doing is making conditions much worse. Old ailments are returning. Even young children are obese. You are needing to think, even though you do not want to think. Self discipline has been lacking in so many for so long, it is not easy to put it back.

It takes effort to use discipline. It takes effort to make your voices heard. You cannot continue as an onlooker. Terrible as they are, catastrophes can pull you up with a jolt, make you act, make you think more deeply.

If you put better fuel into your engines they would work better. You would feel less tired, weary, useless. Eat healthy food, exercise all your moving parts. Raise the tone of your radio, improve the picture on your television screens. You know what I am talking about. I mean watch what is worthwhile. Don't eat the junk, don't watch the junk and above all, see your children raise their sights. Be an example.

Refuse to waste your resources, refuse to use junk items, raise your level to a higher grade in all things. Money doesn't come into this. It will not cost you more; in fact you will spend less.

Notice how boring it is to listen to continual swearing, see continual boozing, hear continual rowing.

Find the pleasure in respecting yourself and respecting others.

Do you ever wonder what you were like in a previous life? Do you ever wonder where you lived before? Who you were? As you are eternal you must have come from somewhere, been somewhere else. Sometimes you get an inkling, a nudge, a premonition. Listen to these signs. They make this present life more worthwhile.

Once you begin to delve into who you might have been, you get curious. Have a discussion amongst your family or friends. Some will tell you to stop talking nonsense. Were they physically blind they would not be able to understand about scenery, clouds, stars. But they are not mentally blind. They just need to start waking up. Remembering who they really are.

This takes pluck. You will be laughed at. Never mind; that doesn't hurt physically. Keep your sense of humour. Sometimes a scoffer will stop you and say, "a funny thing happened the other day. You know what we were talking about? Well, something happened today that made me think it might all be true." And you will have started a ball rolling – and it is going to roll a long way, impossible to catch, but always beckoning you on and on to better, more interesting things. And those things are facts no one wanted to talk about at first try.

Slow to Learn

There is absolute peace at this moment — not a sound. It should be heavenly, but it is not. My mind is a complete blank. I am devoid of questions, feelings, anything. Why? Before going to sleep last night I was full of enthusiasm and questions, ready to get on with this work. Where am I going wrong? I know I am never out of touch with you, dear God, because that is an impossibility for any of us. I know we waste a lot of time thinking about things that do not

11

matter. Worrying about things that may never happen. Living tomorrow that will never come because all is NOW. Now, what is now?

For me it is the beginning of Spring in England. I have just enjoyed a few hours working in my beloved garden. No Your garden. You have lent it to me for my pleasure; it is Your Power that is causing the plants to grow, after their winter rest. Elsewhere in much of the world there is terrible conflict; death and destruction I can hardly bear to think about. Useless fighting, just for possession of land.

You say all is movement. Where is progress?

You have just been watching progress, progress all over your garden. Life Being.

Yes. And here I suddenly find a paradox. I have been pruning – cutting back to force new growth. How about the intrusion of plants into their fellow plants – aren't they wanting more space than they should have, choking their neighbours, encroaching beyond their boundaries? And aren't I forcing my Will on theirs?

In the first instance, you cut back to make room for new growth; you cut away the old wood; you cut out last year's spent branches to make way for New Growth. Secondly, you prevented some plants from harming others, but you did this with love and understanding for the benefit of all. You did not burn them away or poison them away or shoot them away! Do you remember us talking about plants having feelings. They can feel your love and you have learned to feel theirs. All was done for the benefit of all.

When your cities get overcrowded, you do not shoot some of the people out of the way. More houses are built to save congestion. All is progress, movement, Thought in action.

But it doesn't always work that way. Some places are terribly overcrowded. And how do we 'prune' our traffic, clear our airways, make room for all the sick in our overloaded hospitals?

You know the answers to all these questions. You have read about the solutions. That is what I am trying to impress upon all of you through these and similar writings. You, most of you, do not want to think so deeply, yet so simply.

I know what you, yourself, think when you see the vast amount of clothing in your stores, the enormous servings of food in your restaurants, the unbelievable variety of cosmetics and lotions and potions in your shops. You think of the starving and the homeless. Remember they do not clamour for these things in abundance – they need very little to make their lives better. Recall what you read about that tribe of Aboriginals, living in harmony with the plants and animals – and happy.

When you learn to share there will be more than enough of everything – more than enough room, food, clothing, space. You do not need half of what you have, yet how many people are satisfied? Your legs are for walking, your hands are for making. And since you are all One, your goods and your thoughts are for sharing. And when you live thoughtfully, using your free gifts, you will become healthy in body and mind.

How many people do you know who are full of joy?

Strange you should ask that. I encountered a young man today who gave off great joy and he was engaged in trying to promote help for Dr Barnardo's. He was doing charity work and his joy was infectious and his ideas, during my short conversation, were great. He literally jumped for joy as I left him because he was going to buy one of your books – ' Good God'! So my answer is – I know very few people who are full of joy and, oh God, how they stand out.

Two hours have now passed since I thought my mind was a blank!

Finding the Way

I have been wondering how we can find our way out of the mess we are in. Suddenly it is clear that we have written our own Tragedy, with villains, swindlers, pretenders, murderers, tricksters in the cast – and there is no happy ending. We have been enacting this play for centuries. We have been watching the rich lording it over the poor; the powerful enforcing their ideas. In the West we have removed the death penalty and the taking of slaves. Or have we? That is done in a more subtle way now.

It is time to write a new play; a super Musical with a Happy ending – except now we know there is no ending. It is time to sift through the past stories; to remove all the illusions, the cruel scenes; the senseless and useless dialogue. And, very importantly, to remove all the lies about God and what man thought He wanted and demanded.

We do not have to discard all the players, nor change all their parts; rather we should regard that as history, from which we can learn and we can give better parts to those who went unnoticed before.

This new story can be enacted in our present buildings – we have the beautiful churches, mosques, synagogues already there. But now the congregation can choose who will take the leading parts. In fact, all that pomp and ceremony and 'dressing up' will not suffice for this new play; nor will the people looking on need to wear black, cover their faces, bow their knees and their heads, chant repetitious noises.

We shall start flocking to all the free seats; we shall not require prayer books. We shall go to hear wonderful speakers who are a little ahead of us in explaining the Truth and what the Real God says. How he speaks within us at all times, yet demands nothing but Love and needs nothing from us. In fact he doesn't demand Love, he demands nothing for he has All and has given us All. We are just so slow to realise it.

We shall like to hear about the great souls from the past. We shall listen to the exemplary stories about their lives, devoid of the trimmings man has added. We shall never tire of hearing about Jesus and his earthly mission, more about Mohammed, the Buddha, etc. and further of recent examples like Mother Theresa, Nelson Mandela, White Eagle (through Grace Cooke), and writings through some of our other great mediums.

The true meaning of Spiritualism will be understood and no longer feared as mixing with the devil – who does not exist anyway.

And the music! Oh, it will fill our whole Being with such deep joy and thanksgiving.

So, is all this fantasy?

Dear God, have I just been day-dreaming?

Child, you have been portraying your future. When enough of you get together and start putting these dreams into reality you will know the Golden Age has commenced. I have reminded you before, from little acorns great oak trees grow. Jesus said, "when two or three are gathered together in my name (meaning God's name) you shall do these things, and greater than I" and you once mentioned what an astounding statement that was.

Truth is spreading and there is no vaccine that man can produce that will kill it off. It is strong and once it enters your mind and your body no one and nothing, no thing, can eradicate it. It not only reaches every cell of your body and mind, but it brings strength, endurance, health, happiness and it is immune to dying.

The buildings you have been talking about will become filled with Light. They will become a magnet. You will give of your time, your income, your energy and you will do it so lovingly that it will 'rub off' on the very fabric of the buildings, causing them to need less repair; they will no longer decay. They will become more like the buildings you have read about on the next plane – your heaven world as you name it.

Dream on – and on. Dreams come true because you are seeing the finished article, then working out the details, ready for the work to commence. Remember that order, which I keep reminding you about?

Belief

What is the difference between belief, knowledge, imagination and wisdom?

You can believe that you have knowledge and you can imagine that you are wise. You can know that you are using your imagination and you can believe that you are without wisdom. You can use imagination and wisdom and you can acquire belief and knowledge. You can 'play' with these words until they mean everything or nothing!

In Truth you have all these things. How you use them is up to you. Deep within you is all knowledge, all wisdom and a sure belief of the Truth, and at all times you are using your imagination to understand this. Imagination is another word for 'seeing'. Imagination puts your words into understanding.

You can believe that something is, or is not, true. You can imagine that something is, or is not, right. But you cannot KNOW deep within that something false is true and Wisdom is that knowing. You cannot KNOW deep within that something true is false and Wisdom is that knowing.

Phew! That wants some taking in. I 'Know deep within that this is Truth', but I must keep re-reading this to see if I can find a mistake – yet You do not make mistakes! I suppose it is the 'little I' that wants to look for faults that are not there. I mean false sense.

This makes me think about the interpretations of the Bible, the Qur'an and all other religious writings. It is more about sorting out the wheat from the chaff. Our inner knowing can sort out the Truth.

Your inner knowing is your connection with Me. You, yourself, know when I am talking to you. You still 'imagine' me as a person and you still 'hear' me as a voice. There is nothing wrong with doing this. It is your way of understanding and of passing on your understanding to others.

15

We will go back to the beginning – you are using your imagination to put down what you believe to be true and that requires knowledge and wisdom!

Yes, but this is where I sometimes query my interpretation of what you are telling me. Someone much cleverer than I might come along and tell me what I have just written does not make sense.

Someone much cleverer than you possesses the same inner KNOWING of Truth – no more, no less. Someone much cleverer than you may not have the same belief nor even as much wisdom! For here you are talking about 'clever' in an academic sense. How you all use your belief, your imagination, your knowledge, your wisdom is up to you.

*Yes, I see your meaning; being an academic doesn't mean being able to grasp this kind of simple Truth. In fact, it can be a deterrent to understanding simple Truth, just because it **is** simple. You said the other day, YOU are simple. I like that – it helps me to remain without awe of You. Oh, dear God, how complicated man makes Life. The little starving Africans, the uneducated Indians, the sick Iraqis can understand this simplicity if only we will help them, and not preach to them, especially about hell and damnation.*

This brings me to thinking about what happens to them when they pass over to the next plane. I have learned that we find ourselves where we expect to be. Now I can understand that those without belief in a further Life, find themselves in a kind of nothingness until they start to 'wake up', but what of these innocent souls who have not had the privilege of being given the chance to think at all?

They too have that inner Knowing. It may seem dormant, but remember their life on this earth plane is not their first life. Where have they come from? Did they choose to incarnate into their present state? And if you think they do not have the answers to these questions, remember there are thousands of loving souls 'on the other side' waiting to greet them with great love, great compassion, great understanding. What a wonderful awakening they will experience.

That comforts me.

My Vision

My vision of the Golden Age is of an earth plane without violence, without envy, without hatred, without cruelty. All peoples will be satisfied with their life and find satisfaction only in helping others.

Work will have a different meaning. There will be no work for reward. Work will have become a 'hobby'. And the work that we now look upon as horrible, dirty work, will be shared by all, just as all the satisfying and worthwhile jobs will be shared.

Children will be guided right from babyhood to be kind and thoughtful. Instead of adults saying, 'don't do that', 'be quiet', 'stop shouting', children will hear 'be thoughtful', 'be loving', 'come to me and I will explain'. They will play, but they will not fight. I picture parents teaching little groups of children in their own homes and taking it in turns each week, or even each day.

Then there will be nearby fields for children to play with plenty of parents and other adults joining in. There will be small buildings where potters work, where many kinds of hand crafts are carried on, and pools to swim in. Children will Choose to watch and to learn what interests them most. They will Choose to take part.

There will be beautiful 'Halls of Learning' as there are on the next plane. These will attract those young people who wish to study certain subjects deeply. There will be willing teachers there to help them. These Halls will have replaced out present Universities. There will be no requirement to go there if your desire and ambition is to become a gardener, a builder, a carpenter. In those instances your place will be at the site of current similar work, watching and learning from 'masters of their trade' who will find great joy in teaching a willing pupil.

Recreation will be at discussion groups; listening about the work of others and also listening to the thoughts and ideas of others. Travel will be possible all over the world because a different form of journeying will have been discovered. 'Wise Ones' who are more advanced will be recognised and respected. A feeling of love and unselfishness will abound.

There will be no stealing, for what would be the point? There will be no cruelty, and animals will be very much a part of everyone's life – but not to kill and eat. We shall live off the land, nourishing our bodies with uncontaminated, simple food that will have regained its original wonderful flavours. There will be many games, but not competition.

All this seems rational to me, for surely this is the after life we are heading for now? But then I think of paedophiles and my house of cards collapses.

What of those, dear God?

Paedophiles in Heaven?

Do you think there are paedophiles in Heaven?

Well, not actually in Heaven, but I understand such depraved souls, along with murderers, perverts, drug addicts, find themselves in a sort of 'murk' until they begin slowly to 'wake up'. On earth now, we imprison them.

And does that cure them?

Usually, I believe, not.

Do you think there will be psychiatrists in the Golden Age?

Yes, probably, along with many kinds of therapists, homeopathic doctors, scientists, astrologers and astronomers.

And isn't it your present belief that these people are able to help your fellow human beings more than imprisoning them does?

Yes.

And isn't it your present belief that most of humanity's ills and disasters are caused through lack of correct training, teaching, example?

Yes.

Since you started to put into words your Vision, you have read some helpful passages in one of the White Eagle books. You are grasping more Truth. You are forgetting that this Vision brings Me, Good, God, much more noticeably into your daily lives.

There will not be boring, monotonous religious Services, that brush off on the congregation like fluff in a breeze. There will be Great Speakers whom you will flock to hear. What they say will not brush off on you; their message will sink deep into your very Being. You will receive food for thought, food that you will wish to discuss with others, put into practice, spread around. And it will not seem boring! As I said to you recently, dream on – for this is the stuff of reality. The building blocks are getting ready to be used.

Scattered Seed

The Rose is bright flame colour, fully open, and has become a close-up, filling the whole frame of my 'picture'. What does this mean, God?

Now a shadow has come across it, causing it to lose its colour; now it has gone. And what is in its place? You are seeing a grey, stony, flat scene that meets the horizon. The stones are bright and the sky is blue but the vibrant colour and the wonder has gone.

I am disappointed. I thought there was about to be a wonderful episode in our story – no not story, for what you covey to me is the Truth. Now the scene is empty. Not grey and lifeless, but flat, a nothingness. What does this mean?

Remember the Bible story about some of the seed falling on stony ground? The seed has fallen here, but it has gone between the stones, it has met with no response. The stones are dry, hard, apparently unfeeling. But, I tell you, the seed is there; it has dropped down out of sight, but it is there. It is not very far below the surface, not too far for a little light to penetrate and when the rains come the water will trickle below the surface. That will make the little seed stir.

The seed may lay dormant for a long time, but it will not die. It awaits warmth, encouragement. It is putting down tiny roots because further down is nutriment.

There is movement below the surface. Ashes begin to cover the stones, ashes from an earthquake far away. The stones do not like this coating of dust, they feel smothered, until rain comes down and washes in those ashes. They in turn cover the seeds and the little seeds recognise a nutrient, a saviour. They respond with upward growth now. They come into the sunshine they knew was there. The scene becomes 'alive'. Nothing was lost, only covered up.

Now will you liken this to the words of Truth as they fall on deaf ears, stony hearts, resistance. Then, one day, in a quiet moment of meditation, the words begin to make sense. They surface. Soul meets soul. Warmth feels warmth. Singleness becomes Oneness, oneness with all else.

God, what a strange episode this is. I felt so elated when I saw that bright, wondrous flame rose; then all was bleak. Is this the bleakness I myself sometimes feel when your Truth is ignored?

Liken this to the droplet of water that becomes a lake. There is no Time. But slowly, in your idea of time, this seed, this droplet, this Truth is seeping into humanity. The seed is already there, deep within, often so deep that it goes unrecognised, unnoticed, but it IS there. You ARE waking up.

Are more of us now Awake than Asleep?

You all have the same opportunity to Wake Up – from peasants to parsons, from kings to footballers.

It just seems too slow to be in time to save us from ourselves.

All who read these words, go deep within and get to KNOW that seed. It is strong, it is imperishable, it is Life with a capital L. Your Life. Use it, live it, spread it around. Feed it with all the knowledge you can find. Talk about it, yes talk about it. Display it by being joyful. Let nothing get in the way of its progress. Recall that KNOWING we talked about. I AM within you. Are you going to let others see Me? Are you going to feed and water Me? Bring Me out of the shadows into the Light. That Light is you and Me personified, glorious, scintillating Joy, wanting for nothing but recognition.

Know that with every breath you take, every step you take, every thought you think, I AM with you. It is ME that is giving you that movement. All is movement, nothing stands still. Make all your movements towards the Light. That Light is Life, Love, God. You are IMPORTANT.

Despondency

Dear God, I am tired – mentally and physically; I am disappointed, disillusioned. I have written like this in the past. World conditions are the worst part of my depression. There is death and destruction in so many places – where is progress?

You are being the little You. Where is the positivity you talk about when trying to help others? You are having a grovel in the mud. Will that get you anywhere?

No, but I am tired. It is cold and grey this April day and that is how I feel. Is it wrong to feel I have had enough of this particular life?

You are no use to yourself nor to others while you let negativity take over. You know you, and everyone else on the earth plane, leave it at an appointed time. What is the point of letting go of the 'life line' now? You have been praying for many people you know who have 'lost their marbles' as you call it. You ask for them to be returned home – as much for the sake of their carers as for themselves.

Yes. I know I have asked about them before, but I cannot remember what you said!

And in your present mood you cannot be bothered to look up the answer! You have even chosen to type in blue today. To suit your mood I wonder?

Well, isn't that better than black?

Touché, point taken. But what have you just done to get us back on black?

I don't know! And I don't think anyone will believe this is a serious talk with God!

It doesn't have to be serious all the time to talk to Me. Do you not think fun and wit are gifts from God? That belief in solemnity is some of the trouble in many of your religions. You do not find the Truth better by being straight-faced. Remember I once told you – do smile, all of you, you look so beautiful when you smile.

You can see your golden rose still upright. Use it. You are part of all that killing when you are praying for Peace. You are joining with those frightened souls; your love and faith is rubbing off on them, even though you cannot see it, do not believe it. You, all of you who are thinking deeply, need to be fighting for peace; fighting in your hearts and minds, firing love, not guns. Dropping love, not bombs. I WILL KEEP ON SAYING PRAYER IS SO POWERFUL, THOUGHT IS SO POWERFUL. If you are tired of hearing it, put it into practice so that it becomes natural to use this Power. Where is the warring fighting getting you?

You can remember how Pacifists were despised, even punished, in the second World War. Wouldn't your world be a wonderful place if everyone now became a Pacifist!

Oh dear God, what a wonderful thought. What a truly wonderful world it would be if everyone refused to fight. But common sense tells me that is an impossibility because there would always be the few who persisted in fighting and then others would not be safe.

I said, wouldn't your world be a wonderful place if *everyone became a Pacifist.* What is stopping that?

Greed; wanting what is not ours; jealousy; envy.

So in whose hands is the answer?

Ours. It is in the hands of each one of us. It is in our thinking and our acting and in our way of living. You have given us Free Will and we are like children playing with fire – we do not know how to handle it. Instead of using it for warmth we are using it for destruction.

Strange. This talk, although stating grim facts, has given me a fillip to carry on working in my own little way, knowing I am a tiny cog in an enormous wheel. I think of that wild duck in my garden, sitting on her eggs in spite of my noisy lawn mower right near her. She must have been terrified, but she didn't desert her nest. What an example.

Reincarnation

Can we talk about re-incarnation? To me it makes complete sense; to some others it is unacceptable.

Once you really believe there is no death, why should there not be reincarnation?

Exactly. We move to somewhere else when we leave our present body, so there must be other lives to live, other places to go. From much reading I have done on this subject I understand that the usual period of time between reincarnating back to this earth plane is about 300 years, but I also know it can be quite quickly.

You understand rightly. Your present conception of time makes it difficult to grasp this subject. Since you have lived so many lives on your planet it is not becoming to any of you to hold hate or prejudice against another nation, another culture. You have tried them nearly all!

Yes, that can be a sobering thought and makes racial hatred even worse to encounter. We are fighting people we may have been in the past! Do most of us have an inkling of what we have been and where we have been?

You have a sixth sense that you do not use, or use very little. *You* know you have been an Indian, a North American Indian, an Egyptian. You hold strong feelings of rapport with Italians, Greeks and Welsh. You feel you knew Atlantis. How would you describe these feelings to others?

It is more than an inkling – it is an inner knowing; a strong feeling of oneness with those races and those countries. I do not feel I have been a man, nor do I wish to be a male entity, only in so much as I would like more strength for lifting, sawing, building.

Do you think those abilities may appeal to you just because you have had that strength in the past?

That is a possibility, but it does not make me wish to be a man again.

Why?

Because mostly men find it harder to accept these beliefs. They want to prove everything instead of listening to their instinct. They are too 'down to earth' which makes it more difficult for them to rise up into the ether. I don't mean we women have to be airy-fairy. Most women have a softer side; dare I say more feeling. That is why I don't think a man can understand a mother's love for her children. I am not belittling a father's love, but a real mother's love is fiercely protective, deeply understanding; profound yet not possessive.

Do you think a child loves its mother more than its father?

No. I think it is a different kind of love. I think in a good, stable family, a child feels protective towards its mother and looks up to its father.

Do you think you would have felt differently towards daughters if you had had them compared with your love for your sons?

No. I think in my case I would have had that exceptional rapport with my daughters that I have with my sons. I do not think I am in a position to understand the feelings of other parents in general because I have been blessed with exceptional, caring sons and with the love of two young women who came into my life just like daughters. I also had an exceptional husband who loved me and his children deeply and without jealousy or criticism. I have been so blessed over this.

Do you think Choice came into this?

Yes. Choice of this particular husband in this incarnation. I also believe I chose to have the parents I had and I like to think my sons chose to have us as parents, even though one of them had a different father originally. His 'second' father was his choice, of that I am convinced.

Do you feel you have lived with these souls before?

Yes, very definitely. I believed a very talented medium who said my husband and I had had many lives together, and I feel I know my sons far too well for this to be our only life together. We are deeply 'attached'. We could have been brothers and sisters, father and daughter, master and slave! With the young women who came to look upon me as a mother, I know instinctively there is a great depth of feeling, far more than in the sort of wonderful friendship one has with real but ordinary friends.

When did you start to realise these things?

Not until I started studying the White Eagle Teachings. Immediately I lapped up the idea of reincarnation. I had never heard of karma until then and did not understand what it meant. Then I understood it as a recompense and a paying-back of past life experiences. Now I know it doesn't work quite like that, does it?

There is no punishment as such. *I* do not punish you. You punish yourselves and you choose to do it in your own time. Your natural state is to feel good, to feel happy and content. When you do kindly acts you feel good, contented. When you do unkind, mean, unworthy acts you feel uncomfortable. You want to get back to feeling good. You have a desire to 'put things right'. You Choose to put things right. And if you omitted to do this in one life, you choose to correct it in another life. This is where punishment by Me would not work. You have to satisfy your own self; I cannot do it for you.

Here I can ask about something that puzzles me. Jesus is supposed to have died on the cross to forgive our sins. How did he take them away? I don't think he did. I think he came as an example to us all on how to live and then how to know there is no death.

Jesus came to earth in that incarnation as an Example. He showed you how to live. He spoke Truth. He forgave sins in that he let the sinner know he understood their lapse from grace. He showed you how to forgive others and to think first whether you are not just as 'bad'. He used love, he used example, he used compassion. By letting himself be crucified he went through the 'depiction' of death so that he could prove its false conception.

So he didn't forgive us our sins?

He understood your sins. He enabled you to see your sins. He told you he and I are one. I tell you you and I are One. I know all that you do and think. Your fellow creatures do not know all you think and sometimes thoughts are worse than deeds. That is where you have to forgive yourselves. You have to learn to love yourselves and you cannot love yourselves when you know what is inside you, perhaps hidden from others.

We come back to Choice. You choose to be perfect, be kind, be wonderful, in YOUR OWN TIME. Some of you have made little or no progress during aeons of time; others have learned, remembered, Who They Really Are much more quickly.

I know we go to live on other planets. Do we progress from Form 1 upwards or do we dodge about from Form 1 to Form V and back to Form I?

Put it another way. You spend time learning French, then you learn Higher Maths, and maybe become a great musician, but on the way you have left out Art, History, Geography, so you return to study different subjects, finding your other subjects useful. As you become more proficient you can go on to experience much more exotic things on other planets and that may make you wish to return to this earth plane to pass on what you have learned. Or you may wish to 'oversee' the learning of further education from a higher plane. Or you may wish to 'guide' the earth people from a higher viewpoint.

This is perfect sense. It resonates with all I have tried to learn and absorb over the years. I do hope the readers of this can understand how it spells Truth.

Heeding our Conscience

My conscience tells me I should be tuning-in regularly, but my body and little mind are weary, making all mental and physical actions such an effort. This attitude is against all I have learned and I know that once I contact you, my best Friend, I become uplifted. Only You know all that is tiring my state of Being, the concern that I am feeling for another. Please communicate a good long session that will be a lesson for all those of us who get into these negative moods.

Your rose is upright and full of vigour, giving off strong, positive vibes. That is symbolising the real you. The Real You is the same today, tomorrow and always. The real you is strong, happy, useful, full of life with a capital L.

Don't let the little you pull you down for that will be no help to anyone, including yourself.

You can pray and think with Power for positive outcome. All of you can learn from your mistakes. You can become stronger through adversity.

Look back only as a means of progressing now. All is now and your tomorrow will be your Now when tomorrow comes! When you come to crossroads you have three choices – left, forward or right. There is a 'best way' for you and if you cannot sort it out yourself, with your mortal mind, ask for guidance, knowing that it is there for you. I AM with you, so are your guides and helpers. We do not push you, nor force our will on yours; we guide you for what is best at this time. We can see ahead better than you can, therefore we happily guide you in the best direction.

You do not have to take our guidance. You can go 'your own sweet way', but sometimes that way is bitter. Remember you can go direct from South to North or you can go North via East or West. You have free choice, but we dearly love, yes love, to guide you for your own good.

Open your Mind to guidance. Clear out all the negativity, all the clutter, all the FEAR. There is nothing to fear, but it is so hard for you to accept that.

Be calm yet strong, open yet cautious, firm yet flexible. You are NEVER alone. Isn't that a comfort to you? Never Alone.

Listen to the experiences of others *for* their ideas and experiences, but then open your mind for seeing your path ahead. You never stand still. Sometimes the path ahead is very clear and easy to follow; sometimes it is rough, full of nettles, obstacles, thorns, but there is ALWAYS something ahead.

Do not let fear block your path, for if you go forward in faith and love, knowing that *I* am at your side – nay all around you – you will not take a wrong path.

Test your faith and trust. Know the Truth and that knowing sets you free. Looking back will become a waste of time and energy. All is NOW.

Being Judgmental

I used to think people who read their Bible a lot were a bit stuffy, goody-goody. I was not on their wave-length. Occasionally I would read parts of the New Testament. Now I find myself continually picking up "Good God" which You used me to write, dear God. It has become my Bible for it is so full of down-to-earth, common sense. Everything you have said makes it so clear how we should live, how we should love, how we should consider others before ourselves. If only we would put into practice what you say all would be wonderful – all over your world. Oh, how slow we are to learn.

How can this new, understandable approach reach those who are feeling so righteous and those who are literally shouting out their beliefs, waving their arms about, still talking about a revengeful God, and hell and damnation?

Do you remember how I said one nation needed to be bold enough to say 'no more war, no more armaments, no more armed forces'?

Yes, I realised how wonderful that would be and you said others would be so astounded they would not dare to attack, if I remember rightly.

Peace has to be put into practice, not just talked about. Where is example? Where is true faith, clear understanding, a *knowing* of what is right?

Fear is still your real enemy. You haven't the courage to put this radical idea to the test.

You are afraid of reverting to clean, pure living. You are afraid of not having enough. You are afraid to let go of your current grasping for more.

Some of you are finding 'what goes around, comes around'. Some of you are learning and remembering a great deal of useful information.

Only by giving up Force and using Love will you attain world peace. Only by trusting your innermost Knowing will you find what you are looking for.

I know thousands of us are wishing to live this way. I know millions of us have read Neale's books and can see clearly the right way to go, the right thoughts to follow, the way to attain heaven on earth. But, oh God, I cannot see your Good really manifesting anywhere in enough 'quantity' to make any difference. We seem as far as ever from world peace.

I remember you say we do not see the amount of peace and progress that is taking place. No, I am sure we do not. That makes it so hard to remain optimistic. Couldn't you send us such a great, outstanding Teacher that the whole world would recognise his or her presence? Someone whose Light we could actually see around their earthly body?

You all have a light around your earthly body – it is called your aura – and when you are using your real Being, your aura is bright and those attuned to the spiritual plane can see its brightness.

But that doesn't help us who cannot see auras.

You may not see another's aura, but you can feel it; you know instinctively when you are in the presence of Wise Ones. We come back to how you KNOW the Truth when you are listening for it. I have told you there are many Teachers in your midst and you meet up with them when you are ready and seeking. But who is seeking? What would be the use of language teachers all over your earth plane when so few wish to speak another language?

How many people are you, yourself, finding who wish to discuss this different, fresh approach that you and others are writing about? You made a small attempt this morning with someone you know well, but she does not want to let go of her previous beliefs. She admitted it was difficult to let go of what she had been taught as a child, yet she declared she couldn't read the bible! Why? Because the bible has become 'out of date' for your present world.

Oh, that will cause an uproar. To suggest the bible is wrong in any way just makes some people see red! That is why it is not possible to sell 'Good God' and Neale's books in most Bible Shops and Christian Book Shops. These books are not orthodox enough!

What is orthodox? Is it praying a certain way, acting a certain way? Who made the rules? Did Jesus say you must kneel, wear a cross, cover your head, bare your head?

He gave us the Lord's Prayer, word for word.

Well not exactly your words for words because it has been translated many times. So you have the gist. Your 'Father who art in heaven' is Me, Good, to whom you are all connected. My name is universal. My kingdom is Everywhere and you have the Will to do what is right – I do not make you. Your heaven can be on earth. I have given you your daily bread – meaning you have all you require for your sustenance. You need to acknowledge your trespasses and to forgive those whom you consider trespass against you. Temptation is all around you – I help you to lead yourselves away from it and to resist doing what you know instinctively is wrong. My kingdom is your kingdom and you can experience all its glory. For ever and ever.

Oh, what a statement. I need to stop here to take in this astounding aspect.

A Great Need to Learn

I don't need to tell you I watched "The Children of Abraham" on television last evening, because I have learned you always know all that we do! So you will also know how confusing it is to hear the different interpretations of Truth by Christians, Jews and Muslims. And All think they are right. None wants to change. There was a sign of a little tolerance, but mainly the gaps are vast.

I wish I could visualise a coming together, for without it we shall continue to quarrel.

You think you are not 'getting anything' because you think one of us is not able to tackle this! And you think it is you.

Of course it is me. I feel I have bitten off more than I can chew!

All things are possible with Me because I am Good manifesting.

You need to recognise that, as with your politicians and world leaders, some religious leaders are not suitable for their task.

Recall I have said it is you, the people, who put these beings in high places. It is *your* choice. Some leaders want war not peace. Some leaders preach false doctrines. Often the more they shout the more you follow. You can be very like sheep following a shepherd and not every shepherd is well trained. Then there are the sheep dogs who herd up the sheep with barking and even biting.

You are finding this hard to put down. You are fearful of not hearing correctly.

Yes. Why?

You are experiencing fear in dealing with more seemingly difficult subjects. Although the Truth is within you, reach out for it. Do not doubt. Remember when you are out of your depth you have to swim harder. I will not let you sink. You are needed. You found it difficult to write that. You still put yourself down. I am speaking to the Higher You, not the little you.

You cannot change conditions and circumstances without altering the specifications. You watched the programme about Christopher Wren building St Paul's Cathedral and you learned how he had to alter his drawings and materials to take the weight of the dome. He thought he knew it all until he came to put the building into reality. I have told you, all is movement; I tell you, all is change.

Surely we shouldn't change what we know to be good?

29

You cannot change what is good because good is Me – remember – my other name for God. So you can only change what you thought, mistakenly, was good and now find to be flawed. If you fill a pot with a hole in it, all the contents will fall through. There was a flaw you hadn't noticed. Look into your religions, look into your teachings, look for the flaws. Remove the false conceptions and the Truth will remain. And you know what – the Truth will be so astoundingly clear.

You, all of you over your world, need to want change – change for the better. Take off your blinkers and be open to new thoughts about Me and you, Me and Truth, Me and Oneness. You have a saying, 'Read, Learn and Digest'. How many of you are reading and learning and adequately digesting?

'Many Mansions'

I have been asked what happens to the 'bad' souls when they pass over. I have read about this in other books, but please tell us here for those who need to know and for those who have been brought up to believe in hell.

I have told you already, you find yourselves where you wish to be and for some of you that means in the mire.

Most of you wish for a wonderful, peaceful life where all is sunshine, but not an empty existence with nothing to do. There is always more than enough to do, but you will not experience fatigue or boredom.

You recall that recently we talked about knowing what your conscience is telling you at all times, whether you are a child or an adult.

If you are writing up your accounts and you know beforehand that you have spent more than you have received, you will not expect to find yourselves in 'the black' as you call it. Sometimes there is only a small discrepancy; sometimes there is an enormous difference. Now you know we are not talking about money here. We are thinking about your move on to another plane.

If you are experiencing your seventh heaven, you will not wish, nor expect, to meet thieves and murderers, bullies and perverts.

If you have been a continual drunkard, a child molester, a known murderer, you would feel very uncomfortable amongst a group of advanced souls. You would feel you wanted to creep away, out of the way, into different surroundings. You would not feel ready to listen to thoughts about a completely foreign way of life.

Therefore you CHOOSE to join others of similar ilk. The difference now is that your foul thoughts do not, cannot, materialise. You can stay in this state for as long as you like – there is no time. Your ranting and raving brings no relief. You have lost your power to fight. But in time you wish to change; you tire of this situation.

It is then that you 'let in' a pinpoint of light and there are those souls who have chosen to help you at this point. How much you raise yourself from the mire is again your *choice*. No one makes you move out of the filth and stench, yes stench. Those who come to help you need to wear protective clothing, be it of an ethereal nature.

When you open yourselves to a stirring of 'feeling', light begins to meet light. Your helpers are longing for you to arise; they envelop you with love and light, they hold out their hands to you, beckoning you onward. It is up to you when you will follow.

Iraq

8.5.04

Dear God, you know I have just wiped out the whole of your message. I feel devastated. Nothing happens by Chance so perhaps something I wrote was not correct. I will endeavour to start again.

I am appalled by hearing about some of the American and British Forces torturing Iraqi prisoners. What has happened to human beings? I thought we were a caring race. In World War Two, in Prisoner of War Camps in this country, glass cases were erected, showing German prisoners what rations to expect under the Geneva Convention. And **our** *prisoners were being given cabbage water and scraps in Germany. I know this is true because my husband was in charge of building some of the camps as a Royal Engineer in Eastern Command here in England.*

Are we doing any good in Iraq?

You pressed the wrong key. By pressing the wrong key all is being lost in Iraq. Wrong motives, wrong examples, wrong thinking. Yes, I know you are remembering I say there is no right and wrong, but replace the word wrong with false.

Was entry into that war altruistic? Where is example? Has fear ceased?

Do you know anyone who is completely without fear? There is fear of lack, fear of sickness, unemployment, loss of some kind. There is fear of terrorism, climatic changes, interference with the earth's atmosphere, crops, fertilisation, pesticides, various chemicals......... Some religions will tell you it is all God's Will.

Why would I wish you to fear, to fight, to suffer? Who devised and developed guns, bombs, poisons, seeming lack? Me? No, I have to tell you, that through not using your innate wisdom, your love, your understanding, you chose many false paths.

But what can we, the ordinary souls, do?

You can do what you always do in a crisis. Pray. See Peace materialising. Send out compassion to the oppressed. Remember not all those troops are happy with what they are doing. They need guidance, Soul guidance from a Higher Source. You tap into that Higher Guidance when you pray.

False power frequently enters into the minds of those whom you put in charge, be it in your Governments, Forces or Religions. They chose to 'rule', you chose to let them! You cannot pass on all blame to others. Take some blame and start to put it right by your actions, your words, your thoughts and your prayers.

Again I say, Prayer is so Powerful. Use it. Wise and thoughtful prayer is answered.

Time & Choice

Sometimes we experience the joy of answered prayer. Why is it such a seemingly rare occurrence? I know we do not understand what is best in all situations, but at times there appears to be only one right solution.

You are thinking of the lingering soul you visited this morning who sleeps most of the time. You were unable to awaken her and you wondered if her spirit could hear your words and feel the healing rays you endeavoured to pour into her.

Yes, and I do not feel guilty in wishing her to 'move on', to return 'home' for she is very old and no longer lucid.

She is sleeping, in more than one sense. She is Choosing her present state.

Why? She was a gentle, unselfish woman, yet now causes some of her family distress. Even though she is unconscious of time and often of them, they continue to visit her.

And that is *their* choice. While on the earth plane you all find it so hard to understand there is No Time. Some times seem so long, some time goes so quickly. Depending on what you are doing or experiencing Time varies to you. When you experience a sleepless night the hours pass slowly. Most times you fall asleep without knowing it and awake to see many hours have passed. What happened to that time?

I believe we leave our bodies and go 'elsewhere', living in a different dimension. I have so often 'caught myself coming back into my body'. It is a fascinating experience.

And you, none of you, fear falling asleep, even though you may not be conscious of where you will go. And so with what you call death. You do not know when you take your last earthly breath, but you do know when you awake, be it still on earth or on the next plane. That is why it is so irrational to fear death.

When you take a plane from London to New York or Sydney you know where you are going, you expect to arrive. You are not surprised when you get there!

You do NOT die, you CANNOT DIE.

When you left your previous plane to return to earth, you expected to arrive alive!

That makes me ask about still-born babies or those who live only a few hours or weeks.

That was an experience they chose to experience. You may not wish to remain long on the next plane on which you will find yourself.

You mean I could think, "Oh, I remember being here, perhaps many times, I choose to move on further, or to a different place"?

There are countless things you will remember, recall, choose, experience. There is a Plan you know. Life is not just a haphazard affair!

You can see a pattern now. The pattern will be much clearer as you progress. Those little ducklings were in a shell in a nest recently in your garden – now they are out in the open, experiencing all manner of things they would never have dreamed of while they were inside that shell.

What a lovely thought. So simple, yet it makes such a wonderful picture. We have so much to look forward to. That brings me back to asking why would anyone wish to remain here in limbo?

And that makes me repeat, you do not know what that soul is experiencing.

And that makes me ask again – what about euthanasia?

You have free choice. A few of you could decide to kill off everybody and everything just to get to the next plane! Would you have progressed? Would you have learned? Would you have gained anything?

Evidently not. We would all be where we were, except not quite! Yet I still feel there are times when it would be kinder to 'put someone out of their misery' as we do with our animals.

Now here is an analogy for you. You just thought you had lost all you had typed during the last hour. You felt you would 'do anything' to get it back. You knew from experience that it would not be possible to get my message again word-for-word. You wanted to *go back to get back what you had lost. No one else could do that for you.* Would it have been better to have 'saved' your work more frequently en route?

That is a sobering thought. That is much food for thought Does it mean that we should always try to save and never to end life?

The paradox is that you 'move on' when you are destined to move on, whether it be by what you call nature, accident or intent. Nothing happens by Chance!

So we haven't really got free choice?

You have free choice to do what you think is right.

How provocative!

Equality

Will there ever come a time when we no longer have rich and poor, when all are equal?

That condition already exists on other levels of life. Do you remember I once asked if you thought there was money in heaven?

Yes, I remember well and the idea was preposterous!

Why?

Because we shall have all we need.

You have all you need now, but you do not believe that fact. You do not need more, but you think you want more. You are missing out on the joy of giving and sharing. You talk about most things except your money. That is mainly a taboo subject. A certain amount of shame comes into this – either because you know you have too much or because you feel at a disadvantage by not having what you think is enough.

Yes, I know you are thinking about the starving. They would not be starving if you used your resources wisely. You can show the deprived how to live – not in mansions in cities – they need to understand, by example, how to grow their food, how to access their water, how to build shelter, how to work.

Education is available to all in some form. In your Western World education is called Compulsory and that deters the lazy. In Africa and India have you noticed how keen the children are to learn?

You can be happy without jewels and gold; you can be miserable in a castle built of marble. You are all equal, but you are not all the same. A teacher needs pupils; pupils need a teacher. A patient needs a doctor; a doctor needs patients.

Being without a home in the desert is quite different from being without a home in a cold city. You have lived in Africa in peace time; you lived in London in war time. You experienced loving and giving in both circumstances. You shared, all of you. You shared fear in the blitz; you lived from day to day. You shared your food, your little perquisites. Conditions brought out your compassion; conditions made you feel more equal. In Africa you witnessed selfless help given in a school and selfless help given in teaching adults to sing and act. Joy was given and joy was expressed by those who received help and encouragement.

We seem to have lost the art of experiencing real joy. We think our television is essential, yet when we go away we do not miss it. We find different joy in mixing with others, exchanging views. How long is it going to take to make our earth plane a happy place?

It will take until more of my children wish to live lovingly, thoughtfully.

Contact with God

God, what difference does it make when Muslims kneel right down and touch the floor with their heads, when Roman Catholics cross themselves, when Jews wear little caps and pray at the Wailing Wall?

My children have been taught by man, men, to do these things. Bringing you down to your knees, bowing, kneeling, making signs, was thought, and is still thought, to make you subservient to Me. I do not require your subservience. I do require your attention. You already have my attention. You need to quieten your busy little mind to enable you to use your higher mind.

These movements you ask about can be a distraction, but when they become a habit they can help you to raise your thoughts – but they are not necessary! Be STILL and KNOW that I Am GOD.

You do not bow to feel Love, to hear harmony, to see beauty. My Spirit is within you at all times and it surrounds you at all times. Walk into a field and pick a wild flower; look deeply into its construction, its colour, its shape, its allness. You do not bend its stalk downwards to do this – you gaze into it.

That is what I am doing to you and you and you. I see your beauty. You are all the same yet all different. Realise I am the same *to you*, whether you be white, black, red or yellow; whether you be Japanese or Russian. Do you think you are treated differently according to your status, your colour, your race? Do you think you will be segregated in your next life?

I don't, but there are many who believe we cannot go to heaven unless we do, say and believe certain teachings. I was told personally that I am not fit to write about you in this way. And that person said he would pray for me for a week!

Won't he be surprised to meet you!

I hope so! And I hope I shall have the grace not to say, 'I told you so'! Why are men more stubborn than women, generally speaking?

Male stubbornness can be a form of protectiveness towards the female gender just as female compliance can be a form of affection. These traits can be misused, used out of proportion. There is a fine line between love and domination. The essence of Love is selflessness and then that becomes a receiving as much as a giving. You can experience this even with your pet. You give but you do not take, yet you receive.

It would almost seem that the lack of words creates this perfection.

36

Your tongue is a dangerous tool. It can cause more pain than a dagger. A dagger can be withdrawn from the body, but words cannot be withdrawn from the soul. Think well before you speak, before you act, before you judge, before you condemn.

Do not stop to kneel, nor bow, before you contact Me. A split second can save a lifetime of regret.

My children, you Are my children whether you be sage or student, you do well to remember Who you Are and Why you Are and Where you are. Bless you.

God Speaking

God, as I focus this day I don't like the dark red flowers I am seeing, beautiful as they are, for they seem to be portraying bloodshed. When I try to change this picture to the gold rose, the rose stands upright with all the dark red flowers at the base of its stem like a carpet. What is this telling us?

The Golden Light is there; it is always there above the turmoil and bloodshed. Yes, this is showing bloodshed over so much of the earth plane. My People of all races are fighting, and for what? Is *any* good coming out of all this quarrelling?

Not until every nation truly wants peace, truly demands peace, will there *be* universal peace. What are you quarrelling for? It is the same old story of wanting what is not yours, of wanting to control others, of wanting others to conform to your ideas.

You are satisfied to have too much when your neighbour has too little. You even take from those who already have less than you do. Few of you are blameless.

But what can we, as individuals, do. We know so much is wrong, but our voices are not heard.

Your voices are heard to a certain extent, but you need to care more, to think more deeply, to feel more responsible. Too many of you 'live for the day, blow tomorrow'. Do you know that if every soul on earth prayed for Peace for one minute there would be Peace. Think about that. Every soul for one minute. But it would need to be sincere and meant; a cry from your hearts.

Now I know that you know this is unlikely, but change the numbers and the time. If half of all souls prayed for Peace for three minutes there would be a sudden shift in your earth conditions.

This, too, you know is unlikely at the moment, but now realise that if a few million souls prayed every day or night for half an hour of your time Peace would start to materialize.

Oh, you think, millions of people are praying for peace because if you add all the different religions together there must be millions praying every day. But how many are praying unselfishly, unbiasedly, lovingly?

You find time to do other things every day; things that give you pleasure like entertainment, betting, dancing, sleeping, conversing. You do not spend every minute of your day just working; there are gaps. So don't say people do not have spare time.

You, yourself, were once told to find just ten minutes every day to rest and you did not do it. In retrospect was it impossible?

No, it would have been difficult, but I could have made more effort.

To those of you who do find this time now, do not be despondent. Much good is happening, more than you realise. When you pray for Peace, pray also for all my people to think more deeply, pray for them to listen for Truth, to enjoy and appreciate all that is around them.

If you do nothing, nothing happens. If you do something, something happens. Your preachers, your leaders, your teachers, need to help you to think, yes THINK. And think well and carefully, not just for the moment but for the future.

Here is a paradox – ALL IS NOW, but it is up to each one of you to make tomorrow NOW and then yesterday and tomorrow will be as NOW.

Make a reality of your good thoughts. I keep telling you your thoughts are so strong. Those of you who doubt My presence in you, do what Neale (Neale Donald Walsch) is doing, what Betty, this writer, is doing. Tune-in, knowing that if you do it with true faith and inner knowing, you will hear my voice in your head. Listen. Ask, then quieten your mortal mind, and listen. You WILL receive something, be it just a nudge, a sentence, a happening.

Here I say to my readers – try it, it works. You will not be left without proof if you ask from your heart where all knowledge already is. I call it 'satisfying magic' that still seems too good to be true. But it is just that, too good to be true to our earthly way of thinking. Oh, do help to make this lovely earth plane more like the heaven it was meant to be.

Using Thought

I was reading a wonderful article this morning about Affirmations and how powerful they are. God, will you please enlarge on this subject.

By now, having read this far, you know how powerful Thought is. Thought is not only powerful when you are praying and concentrating, you are using it every minute of your waking hours.

Let us use a simple analogy. You divide your rubbish into three lots. Some things are useless and you throw them out. Some things are suitable for composting and putting back into the soil. Some things are worth keeping or sharing or giving away.

You spend much time on rubbish thoughts – the kind of negative thoughts that get you nowhere, leave you doubtful, meandering. Some thoughts are worth putting into the conscious memory box for further use when needed. Then there are the good, strong, positive thoughts that not only go into your conscious memory, but sink into your inner knowing, there to remain and recall for ever.

Every time you affirm that all is well now, that you are satisfied, that you are happy, that you are loved, that you are strong in endeavour for good, all these thoughts become reality. The mortal mind 'gets you down', the immortal mind 'lifts you up'. No one can take away your thoughts. Only you can discard them. Only you can retain them.

You will catch yourselves many times a day being negative. Push that away. Immediately replace it with a positive thought.

Before you read that article, you were rather 'down', concerned, worried. That article lifted you up and you said your daily affirmation several times, thinking about each word. 'I am happy, healthy, wealthy and wise'.

My children, how ever hard your lives may seem, the best way to help yourselves is to KNOW you are always loved, nurtured, alive, able. Able to read if you cannot hear, able to see if you cannot hear, able to hear if you cannot see, able to think though you cannot move. Keep finding the positive. For though you may be suffering, dwelling on it does not make you better, in fact it holds up the process of healing.

Count your blessings, there are more than you realised. Then pray that others may become aware of their blessings and more ready to share them.

Why do you think the heaven world, the summerland, the next wavelength or whatever you like to call it, will be so good? You do not picture illness, poverty, terrorism, lack, fear. Why? Because deep down you know these negative things are of the earth, earthy. They are man-caused.

But do not think you, yourself, will be changed in the twinkling of an eye. It is your surroundings that will be that way. You, yourself, could join with others who still wanted to quarrel, to fight, to control. But, as I told you recently, you will find you have no power for those 'attributes'. They will get you nowhere. They are getting you nowhere now, but it is taking you so long to realise it.

Do not say 'I will' and 'I want', 'it will be' and 'I wish'. All is now. You ARE and you HAVE now. If someone tells you you are a misery or a menace, think about it. You must be giving off miserable or menacing thoughts. You can do something about that. You can alter your thoughts.

We are back to affirmations. You are happy, You are peaceful, You are what you think. Think, think, think about this. Be happy, be peaceful, be grateful, be thoughtful. And when you make this a reality you will attract happy, peaceful, grateful, thoughtful people to you. You become as a magnet.

You cannot hide your Light once it shines. Others will see it and those who cannot actually see it will feel it. When you polish your brass and silver, when you clean your widows, more light reflects. You cannot stop it. Make sure you clean your mind, polish your inmost, remove the layers of fog and rust and mould that have accumulated over the years. You are a beautiful, shining object, priceless yet useful, perfect but with the flaws that helped you to become so, to realise how to help others to obtain perfection.

Remember? You ARE my perfect children in whom I am well pleased because you were made perfect and so you are. Amen, Amen. Amen.

Healing

When we give healing to others, why do we not see the rays or feel the heat from our hands? Do we kid ourselves sometimes that we are actually helping, or does this treatment always happen, even though there are no evident results?

When you work this way with sincerity, from your heart centre, there are always results. You cannot see electricity, you cannot see Love, but you know they are there.

Think of yourselves as being attached to all that is around you. Picture the merest golden threads that not only hold you together, but emanate from you. When you become conscious of this oneness you realise that those threads act as transmitters and receivers. When you study different kinds of healing and therapies you realise how vibrations are picked up. Some healers can realign your threads which have become 'tangled'.

Although you think of many healing therapies as new, they were used in the past, long, long, ago. Nothing is new. You are remembering.

Does the patient need to be in tune with the healer?

No, but it helps if they are aware of what is happening and it helps if they too are in tune with the practitioner.

How about animals?

Remember animals have great intuition and they use their intuition more readily than human beings. They do not doubt. They pick up your moods, their surroundings, an atmosphere. When you love them they trust you. Healing is a transference of Love. Love is everywhere; it is contagious, it is what you call miraculous.

When you think there are no results from spiritual healing, it is because you cannot see, with your mortal eyes, the results on that other soul. Maybe their body continues to manifest in the old way, but their spirit has been touched. You have caused an effect.

Could a bad effect be caused by an inexperienced healer or a vindictive entity?

In these circumstances there is only a nil effect. It would be spoken words or physical pressure that could cause seeming problems. I say 'seeming', because you cannot affect another soul. You can damage another's thinking, but you cannot damage spirit.

When you remember 'My Will be done, as it is in Heaven', you will understand and remember how different earthly life is when your every thought is positive and loving. It is you, yourselves, who hold back your experience of heaven on earth. But you would be surprised how many souls *are* experiencing heaven on earth now.

Try to draw out negative thought from yourself and from others. You pull a thorn out of your skin, your body expels its waste matter. Make sure all you put into your bodies and into your minds is top quality, uncontaminated material. You find that the right people and the right books come to you when you are ready and thousands and thousands of you are absorbing what, to you, seem new ideas, and benefiting from them.

You cannot give too much love away; love and understanding are continually replaced within you at a vast rate. Healing is a great part of Giving and accepting is a great part of receiving. All is motion. All is Now, yet every minute is different.

Wake Up

June 2004

I am not tuning-in to write this section, it is me, Betty, writing, but it is from my heart.

I am trying so hard to reach *your* hearts. I know this is happening to those of you who are seeking the plain, simple Truth. You find the 'right' books to suit your needs, the 'right' people to talk to.

Unfortunately only a very few of those I am trying to reach will read this and *they* will need to remove their blinkers. I am talking to the Archbishops, the Canons, the clergy in general, the Jehovah Witnesses, the Roman Catholics, the Muslims, the Jews, those connected with the recent TV programme called "God is Black", the owner of a bookshop who told me he would pray for me every night for a week because I was so wrong, the man in a Christian Bible Shop who brought me passages from the Bible to prove all that was written in it was the only Truth, the young Muslim girl who felt so strongly the need to wear her Jilbab at school that her case was taken to Court. I could go on and on.

When we really want to find out what Life is all about we need to go right to our heart centre and think. Question why you think how you do, why you believe what you do, could you be following the wrong path because you are following what you have been brought up to believe, and if so where did that belief come from.

Our fundamental mistaken belief is to think that God is a person. God is ALL GOOD. Love is not a person. Love is ALL LOVE. Thought is not a person. Thought is a POWER. Truth is just that, TRUTH, but man has tampered with it for centuries and centuries until, through translations and omissions and additions, the original Truth has become distorted.

How *can* you believe God is a person? He is not white or black or Jewish or Muslim because Good is not any of those things – Good is Good, All Love, All Life, All Power. And God, Good, is in every one of us, equally. Great Masters have chosen to return to this earth plane through the ages to try to teach us this Truth and we have distorted it.

If we were putting this Truth into practice we would not have rich and poor, homeless and starving, fighting and warring. Oh, how far we are from being God's Children. What a bad example we are as Christians, Muslims, Jews, Hindus, Baptists. No Faith has got it all right. There are bits of Truth in most faiths, but so much that is false, man-initiated.

Do you think, honestly, that Good minds whether you wear a crucifix, cross yourself, bow down, wear black, cover your beautiful faces, take off your hat, put on your cap? Doesn't it begin to sound rather silly?

Do you think you are more worthy to 'go to heaven' than the man next door because you go to church and he doesn't? How do you know what *he* is thinking? Do you realise that Thought is your most powerful tool? Thought causes War, Thought causes jealousy, envy, judgment, hatred. Thought also causes Love, Unselfishness, Understanding, Compassion, Enlightenment.

Enlightenment is what we so lack. We all think we are Right and others are Wrong. Good says there is only Right.

How far we are from being unselfish, for if we were so, there would be no homelessness and starvation. There would not be the 'haves' and the 'have nots'.

Are you satisfied with the way you are? I am asking all of you. This includes the righteous, the exalted, the Pope, Royalty, Parliamentarians, Heads of State, Pop Stars, Generals, Prison Governors, Bishops. The list could go on and on.

Obviously Bob Geldorf wasn't satisfied with the way he was and look what *he* did. But we don't all need money to do good. Our Thoughts are what count. Catch yourself thinking. How much of it is worthwhile, without judgment, full of love and understanding. Most of our ordinary thinking isn't worth thinking. Good, positive, strong Thought is POWERFUL. Good Thought is Prayer; Prayer is Good Thought,

43

unselfish Thought. Thought moves out into the ether and joins similar thought and becomes reality. That is why we don't want to think War Thoughts, Fear Thoughts, Revenge Thoughts.

You can find time each day, however busy you may be, to think good, positive thoughts and to make a point of sending them out into the ether to become reality. God, Good, knows our every thought. When you tune-in to this wonderful Friend you receive comfort, love, guidance.

I have been reading part of Louise Hay's Book "You Can Do It" about affirmations. They work. Not only do the positive ones work, unfortunately the negative ones work too! Tell yourself you are miserable, unloved, useless, and you will be so. You will continue to be so until you alter your thoughts. Tell yourself you are loved, capable, efficient, intelligent, and you become so. You are already all the positive things, but you forget to remember.

I have been re-reading an old book called "Lychgate" by Air Chief Marshal Lord Dowding, written about sixty years ago. I quote from it, "Prayer is only Thought aimed in the direction of God. .... For thought is real, thought is dynamic, thought does things, thought moves mountains......"

What a terrific responsibility we each have, for by our thoughts we fashion or destroy our world. How many of us try to fashion our world? These days, how many of us try to educate our children in their way of thinking?

When my mother was young she was taught about hell fire and brimstone. After a good, unselfish life, she asked me, when she was very old, "You don't think we go to hell, do you?" Poor darling must have been wondering about that all her life! When I was young my religious upbringing was an occasional visit to a Church of England (when if unlucky, it was the first Sunday of the month when we kept saying "We beseech thee to hear us Good Lord" and I used to think how bored God must get with that) and Divinity lessons at school, taken by the headmistress who kept picking up pieces of chalk from the floor. Each weekend we had to learn a Collect.

Now, children either never hear God mentioned, or they are taught all in the Bible is correct, or in the Qur'an or whatever book with which their parents wish to indoctrinate them. Things haven't changed very much. No wonder we still have wars. And we dare to call ourselves civilised!

So, please, please Wake Up. Think deeply. Question your beliefs. Read enlightened books. Pray with your Thoughts. Know that there is a wonderful Light shining down upon our earth. Hold our earth and ALL its inhabitants in that Light so that Peace and Love may manifest EVERYWHERE. God blesses you all the time. Absorb that Good.

Soul & Spirit

Dear God, I have received a question which, though I feel I could answer it myself, I know you will do so accurately. Please come through me again.

What is the difference between Soul and Spirit?

You have just used your symbol of the pink rosebud on the grey velvet in the gold frame as if it were the cover of a book, and when you opened the book, what did you see?

Nothing, just blank pages.

And what does that mean? They were pure white pages without print. All were the same.

Does that mean that, as I thought, there is really no difference between Soul and Spirit – one is just part of the other?

Yes. A grain of salt or a grain of sand is part of a vast quantity of the same thing. Only a small amount is required for a certain purpose, but it is no different from the whole.

You are all one Spirit and part of the individual You is divided up, leaving one part here on this higher plane and part of You is in and around your earthly body.

When a child builds a sand castle it erects a small amount of the whole into a little mound, which is still part of the beach; then when the tide comes in it all gets washed back into the whole.

So with what you call death, the part of you you call your Soul returns to its Source and becomes Spirit, still with an individuality, but part of the Whole.

You on the earth plane are surrounded, enclosed, enveloped in Spirit, yet each one of you is different, (but not apart) in what you and we call Soul.

You and I are one in spirit.

Does it help to say you love your child or your pet and that love is surrounding it, but when you pick it up and cuddle it or press it against you, that love impregnates it. By doing this you take nothing away from your original love, you are just individualising it.

This happens when you love the flowers and they love you back, which you yourself know; nothing is diminished, it is just made manifest.

Spirit, Soul, true Love are all one. All is held in perfection by the Whole which is all three.

Making Ourselves Work

God, I cannot understand my reluctance to tune-in lately. I am devoid of questions, but I wish to 'spread' your words, for the world so badly needs them.

Is it not symbolic for your work that you keep an artificial rose, named Peace, in a specimen vase right by your computer? You cherish the fact that you live in peace; you desire peace; you create peace. You are greatly disturbed by the continued warring in Iraq, the disturbances in many countries and the scenes of the starving and homeless in many places.

You are letting these conditions affect your thoughts and your resolve. This is happening not only to you, but to thousands of others who work for Peace.

Be an example, all of you who are striving for peace to manifest. Do not be affected by those who say, "it is hopeless, there will never be world peace, there will always be fighting and wars". You know better than that.

I keep telling you, Pray Peace, Be Peace, Know Peace. I am not saying Pray FOR Peace – there is already Peace for the taking. It is there, everywhere, like air, light, rain. You cannot stop it, but you interfere with it.

You can pray for man to *want* Peace, for man to become enlightened. Do not listen to those who say 'it will never be'. Of course it will never be if you believe that.

You get what you believe. Just for a moment, instead of knowing that you are All One as I tell you, pretend you are all separate. Now be your own little complete world and choose whether you will be Peace or War, Satisfied or Dissatisfied, happy or miserable. You can choose what you are. Then look at the other souls around you and choose which ones you will connect with, which ones attract you. Do you begin to get the picture?

Now apply this *en masse* all over the world. You cannot alter what another has been thinking, believing, practising, but you can try to be an example and a demonstrator and a guidance in their lives. Like attracts like and light shines forth. Jesus said, 'by their deeds ye shall know them'. Light and Love are spreading. It is often difficult for you to see it, to feel it, to believe it, but I tell you it IS happening.

That is why it is so important to watch all your thoughts, your wishes, your actions, your words. You remember I talked about Thought recently by saying THINK, THINK, THINK more deeply. I have given you peace and plenty, it is up to you to receive it and to make sure it is distributed. I cannot do that for you or you would have no free will.

Simple Truth for Simple People

God, do we grow in knowledge by the ups and downs we experience? This week, for me, there have been highs and lows, pessimism and optimism. The latter is the expansion, hopefully, of your book, 'Good God' at last taking place.

One way and another you have been 'pushed' quite a lot in the last few days to get on with your work, to be optimistic, to proceed with deep-rooted ideas. Go for it. There are many on the higher planes giving you encouragement to develop my thoughts that I put through you.

Do you remember you considered calling your last book 'Direct Line to God'? Well, that is what you have developed so you need not feel guilty, thinking you are not using your Guide. Your Guide, like all Guides, wants only for your good and the good of the Whole. He is there and you are often conscious of his nudges, but when you tune-in as you call it, you come direct to Good, Me, the Great I AM.

When you return to the Higher Realms you will meet your Guide and Helpers, you will understand so clearly 'how things work'! Just as now, you know you do not take full advantage of your computer, nor understand its workings, so you will grasp what has been, and is being done with you at the mortal level.

We need simple, unscientific minds to do work for the simple, unscientific souls seeking Truth in their simple ways. It is easier to teach a comparatively empty mind, than one filled with scientific dogma. *You* know how easy it is to contact Me, to hear my Truth, to use my Truth. To you it is easy to make affirmations work, to expect Good, to expect happiness, to experience peace within.

Stay calm in spite of adversity. Use Love in all circumstances. Know the Truth in spite of untruth. I am speaking to all of you. Hear Me.

You are wriggling against what I am now going to say because you still do not truly trust yourself as my mouthpiece.

Oh, God, I am so afraid of misinterpreting your words.

Why? Have you not yet had enough practice? Would I go on using you if I did not trust you?

No. Forgive me. I still feel unworthy. I promise to proceed with arrangements for the other work I now feel duty bound to do.

Now you have forgotten what you did not write down! I was saying you, Betty, like Neale Donald Walsch, are reaching the seekers of all denominations to help them understand the simplicity of Truth. You are writing the New Age Truth. It is simple, unbiased, natural, unadorned. There is no need for edifices, artefacts, bowing, kneeling, chanting, shouting, hushed voices.

I am speaking to all my lovely souls; Muslims, Jews, Christians, Hindus, Baptists, Methodists, Roman Catholics, Plymouth Brethren, Jehovah Witnesses. YOU ARE ALL ONE.

You can follow much of your teaching, but be open to change, to enlightenment. Dig your own piece of land, choose your own plants, but do not try to make your neighbour do exactly the same. Then see the results. Discuss what does well and what fails. Be open to change. Love one another. Be there for one another. Try to understand one another. I have given you Peace but its manifestation is in YOUR hands!

Orthodoxy

I have just looked up the word 'orthodox' and what I glean from the long explanation is that it means currently acceptable, conventional, established. It does not state that it means absolutely Right. In other words, orthodox is what man has tried to make 'right' and 'acceptable' to his way of thinking.

48

No wonder I considered calling this book "Our Unorthodox God" for You, God, do not fit in with what is called orthodox.

It would be inappropriate to call Me orthodox. I Am God – pure and simple, yes, pure and simple. GOOD. Good is Good. Good is not a bit good or a lot good. It is Good – pure and simple. LOVE is Love, not partly Love or massively Love. Love too is pure and simple. Therefore you can say 'God is Love' and 'Love is Good' and 'Good is God'.

Is Good, God personified?

You can put it that way if you wish, but I am not a person. When you stop trying to make me a person you will realise you cannot make Me have rules and regulations. Nor are there rules and regulations for Love. If you live in the essence of Good and Love you become Good and Love; no rules apply.

You were created by Good and Love to be just that, for in Reality there is nothing else. You are a progression. All is movement, all is progress, trying to reach The Now.

Why do you think you are ever reaching out, for that is what you are doing – you are 'reaching for the stars', 'reaching for the moon', living for tomorrow. Instinct is pushing you on, telling you there is more to come, making you want to progress. Whatever you are doing or making or seeking, you want to do it better or make it better or find something better. You are not still, for you are full of Life and your bodies are continually renewing themselves, your cells, your thoughts are moving.

When you have completed learning in the First Form, you move on to Form Two. Very few of you would wish to spend your life in Form One. Therefore, does it not make great sense to you that when you reach the end of your earth life, you move on further? When you leave school, you do not stop learning, even if you do not go on to University or College. Life teaches you. Every Day teaches you. Every other soul teaches you. The animals and birds teach you.

Why would this earth plane be the only place to live?

Exactly. It is obvious it is not, yet so many people fear death. Why?

Would it be because of what they have been taught during childhood – and adulthood – by people who think they know all the answers? That brings us back to your many and various religions. I have told you, there is Truth in most of them, but there is a great deal of falsity. When you wish to change, you change. When you wish to stay where you are, your body keeps changing, but your mortal mind remains stagnant. Stir up a pond and the rubbish comes to the top and you don't like the look of it. Swim in a clear pool and you see the bottom is clear, the Light shines through the water and there are no dark patches. That is Enlightenment. You understand that these examples are analogies.

Cause & Effect (i)

God, tell me something amazing, something that no one will believe!

You are all wrong!

I wasn't expecting that! Surely we are not ALL wrong. What a depressing thought.

I was exaggerating; I was 'putting down' the Know-Alls. I was making you think. For you all think you are right – why else would you behave as you do. Listen to World Leaders, Politicians, Lawyers, Teachers, Church Leaders, Parents, Children. Yes, Children. Do you agree with all they say? If you were right in everything you do, say and think, you would have a perfect world. What marks do you give out of a hundred to being near a perfect world?

I doubt we have achieved 10%. Scientists believe they have discovered something world-shattering, often to find later there were flaws. Archaeologists tell us a prehistoric find is ten thousand years old, only to find it is nearer 100 thousand. Lesser mortals discover plastic which helps save our trees, only to find plastic cannot be destroyed in the ground. Some of us think we are good gardeners, good hairdressers, good drivers, only to find we make some awful blunders.

So where are we going so wrong?

You need to be discovering, concocting, formulating, in order to progress, but that does not make you a perfectionist. Much is done without forethought for eventualities, without thought as to how a discovery will be used in all its forms. When you interfere with nature, you upset balance. When you interfere with another Race you cause discontent and disruption. Coming down to basics – when you eat the wrong food you cause your body to disrupt!

So how can we become more right?

Every act, every thought, needs Love. Yes, you are thinking, try telling that to a group of thugs! Well, if they had been brought up in Love, in

Thoughtfulness, they would not behave as they do. They would be finding pleasure in helping the elderly instead of rage in throwing stones through their windows. They would be wanting to learn about their world instead of drugging themselves and drinking themselves into a kind of oblivion. What has happened to discipline, to self-satisfaction?

You have been re-reading about the Ancient American Indians, how gracious and wise they were, how calm, how trusting in a Higher Intelligence. Can you apply graciousness, wisdom, calm and trust to your world in general?

Can you apply those attributes to anyone you know? They may have some of them, but few have all of them. Therefore there are mistakes, quarrels, misunderstandings and mistrust. Apply that to the world and it becomes catastrophic; you fight each other and distrust each other. Where is Love and Understanding?

And then you were surprised when I said you are all wrong!

But you say there is no right and wrong and that you do not judge.

There is only a Right Way. And I am not reprimanding, judging, punishing you. You do that yourselves. You have Free Will to go your own ways, but where is that way leading you?

God, I wish you would reprimand us, make us go the right way, for we are going backwards.

Backwards? Some of the past was better. You have just mentioned the Ancient American Indians. Grace Cooke has written about them, remembers living amongst them, as did *you.*

How will you progress without Free Will? How would you know great joy without the act of free-will loving and giving? How would you describe the beauty of a sunset without having accepted Love into your heart?

You curse the cold or the heat or the rain if it upsets your plans. Do you stop to think it is just what others may be praying for, for the good of their crops?

But to those of you who are thoughtful, I say do not despair. No good is wasted, no good thought is wasted, no kind act is wasted. Pray for enlightenment for yourself and others, for World Leaders, for *World Helpers.* There are those who give up their normal lives to go to the aid of the homeless and starving. And Tony Budell is one of them, remember?

Feel the good that comes to you from others and feel the good that you give out to others. Build up a great power of good, unselfish, understanding Thought, then send it out into the ether and see it pouring down upon the earth, magnified by me, Good.

Listening

How interesting it is to listen to others. We are often so anxious to impart our own news that we forget to listen.

It is by listening that you progress. That does not mean that what you are hearing is always right, but it means that you are using your Mind to absorb *more* and your Intellect to *throw away* the dross.

When you listen to a debate you realise how you are agreeing, differing and dithering between ideas. A 'heated' debate loses its strength because raised voices and intolerance deflect from the original subject matter.

Often there can be more than one opinion or inspiration or way forward that will work; then you need to think, unselfishly, which idea will benefit the most people.

Sometimes compromise is called for. The calm and thoughtful people make more impression than the boisterous and egotistical.

Not only do you grow from listening, but also from reading. I am not referring to the Press where much is sensationalism, I am referring to writings by deep thinkers. If you have been brought up to read and believe only one 'Holy Book', how can you compare the truths that are in most of them and be able to intermix harmoniously?

An open mind is ready to listen, ready to change an opinion, anxious to learn more. A closed mind denies that others can also be right.

When you realise that it is just as correct to be Jew or Christian or Muslim as it is to be black or white or yellow, you will progress.

Now that last sentence will confuse, annoy or horrify those of you who believe only your way is the right way. As you are ALL part of the Great Intelligence, why should you not all be correct? You do not realise that, through your religion, you are all trying to reach ME, to understand ME, to *recommend* ME.

You are already 'of Me', you already have Me in your innermost, you already know what is best for one another. Yes, in spite of your differing views and opinions and teachings, you *know in your innermost* The Truth. Truth is plain and simple, without rules and regulations, without creed and dogma.. Love One Another. Jesus told you that over two thousand years ago. You are all born with that knowledge. You love your mother, your father, your child, your pet. Your pet loves its young, wild creatures and birds love and nurture their young. Why can you not love one another?

The joy you experience when you love one another is beyond description. The joy you miss when you deny yourselves this experience is very sad.

Step over the border and love your brother in the next country instead of considering him your enemy. Those who were once enemies in past wars can and do become great friends, wondering why they ever quarrelled. Your dog may hate cats, then you accept a cat or a kitten into your household, and dog and cat become caring friends. Oh, my children, your lives can be and are meant to be HEAVEN ON EARTH.

Hasten the New Age of Peace and Love by *being* Peace and Love.

You will all live for ever, for there is No Death, so do not tell your brother man that he will not 'see heaven' unless he believes as you do. Do you think *you* or *I* decide who will live on? I tell you, I decide, and I decided in the beginning, there is no end!

Unorthodox Statements

God says:

1. There is no God! There is only God, Good. Good is everywhere, therefore there is no place for evil, there is no room, no crevice, where Good is not, hence no space for evil.

2. Love your neighbours, no matter how objectionable you sometimes find them, for by so doing you will love yourself for being able to love them. Your neighbour is just as full of good as you are — they just don't realise it and practise it.

3. Now that you love your neighbour, no matter what, you are entitled to love yourself.

4. Love Life for in so doing Life will love you back. Remember about those golden threads that are all around you, connecting you to each other, to Life and to Love and to God (who is not a person, just Good, unbelievably Good).

5. You can afford to feel Good because that is just what you are, so be sure to act Good, to Be Good, to revel in Good. You deserve the best, not second best, because you are perfect, so make sure you act perfect, enjoy perfection and the perfection all around you.

6. Give because you want to give. Receive because your good is coming back to you, pushed down and running over. It never left you. Life works like that.

Because you are Good and Perfect there is no room for bad and imperfection. Could that be why you find imperfection trying to get at you? It cannot find an entry place so it 'sticks' to your skin, your liver, your brain, your feet, making you seem Unperfect, in pain, itchy, irritable, unwell. Your perfection cannot let in less than itself so unreal imperfection is hanging around, trying to get to you.

You believe in fallacy so you manifest untruth. Your little mind does not listen to your real Mind.

What about the loss of a limb, you are thinking. Was that caused by Good? Was it not caused by war, or too fast driving, or not looking where you were going, or believing that the 'bad' (that couldn't get into you) is trying to travel down or up your perfect body?

Now you are wondering about accidents. There are no accidents. Either your 'accident' has been caused by another's carelessness or because the condition in which you find yourself will help you to help others.

Some of you are now confused; some of you wish to argue these points.

Think. Let go of a feeling of superiority. Query some of your previous conceptions.

You will 'come back home' at the end of your present incarnation, in the perfect state in which you left 'home'. You do not know, you cannot tell, why some conditions seem to 'happen'. Some of you begin to work out your present earth life. Yes, it was a 'present' to enable you to perfect your thinking so as to display, demonstrate, live your perfection.

There is no situation in which you find yourself that cannot help you to progress. There is no situation in which you find yourself that cannot be put to some benefit. There is no situation in which you find yourself that is worse than anybody else has experienced. You are never given more than you can bear. You have asked for it at a much deeper level. When you come back home you will see the pattern and you will see if all the pieces of the jigsaw fit together properly. And if they do not, you will wish to return to perfect the puzzle.

Do not be discouraged by these statements. Be grateful that you can read them and can try to understand them. You will not endeavour to understand them if you are not yet ready to absorb them. When they start to make sense, be thankful, be very thankful, because it means you are progressing faster than you thought!

And you, Betty, were compelled to put down your book and healing list at noon, to come and sit at your computer and write this message. Do you *feel* that?

Yes, very much so. It is a new, 'difficult to explain' situation. It is as if I am picked up and moved from one place to another – no argument, no hesitation, only action.

'The Quiet Mind'

31.7.04

Dear God, sometimes it is difficult to stay positive. We have wars, global warming, excessive heat here in England currently; there is starvation abroad, fires and floods. I was told today this is not all man's fault and extreme weather and ocean changes take place every so many thousands of years. How will we cope?

You are survivors at heart and remember, you are *never* alone. Sadly for you, you often turn to Me only when you reach desperation point.

It is true that not all conditions are man-made, but humanity is causing much trouble, much chaos, much death and destruction.

You look on at young children and watch their progress and their mistakes. They often think they 'know it all' and you have to let them learn the hard way. That is how more advanced souls are looking on at you, dear children. Some of you think you know it all and many errors are made which cause ongoing catastrophes.

I will tell you again, Thought is so strong. Use right Thought and honest, unselfish Prayer. Peace and Love are not appearing as the priorities of mankind.

You have agreed that you do not expect wars in the heaven world. There is no need to have wars on your earth plane. I repeat, you are not satisfied and you do not believe that you can be far happier and healthier with much less.

Your lower mind is not at peace tonight and is beginning to block My message. You feel tired and concerned and are not a pure channel for the Higher Mind to use. I never leave you – we will continue soon.

The e-mail I received earlier today has caused uncomfortable ripples in my mortal mind and questions keep popping up about our future earth conditions. I must 'quiet the fretful daily mind' as White Eagle tells us in 'The Quiet Mind'. We are useless when we try to 'work on our own'.

Receiving Help & Knowledge

Dear God, thank you for guiding such loving, helpful, thoughtful people to me over the years. Since you are not a person, but All Good, how does this operate?

As you know, you are part of All Good and as you open yourselves to this concept you become conscious of others who are likewise, who are seeking, who are wishing to use their goodness, their love, and also to receive it.

Much 'work' goes on at a deeper level of which you are unaware and also in your sleep state. You are never 'soul unconscious'. That is why you remember bits of dreams – I say bits because they are usually useless to you. Conversely, there are those who remember much in their seemingly unconscious state and are able to bring it into their conscious mind and write about it.

When we return 'home' will we recall bits of this earth life in a dream form?

Why not? You will do it more consciously from a higher plane, your vision will be clearer and you will see your earth life as a dream.

That is most interesting because it is what was being talked about yesterday and I believe is going to be made clearer to me in a new book I have been given!

There, you see, that is another event that occurs. Books come to you when you are ready to benefit by them. You can read all books at any time, but what you get out of them depends on what stage of 'enquiry' you are at. You know how you can read a book and think you understand it, but sometimes when you read it a few months or years later you 'get much more out of it'.

This is progress my child. All is movement and this includes your thoughts.

Can unkind thoughts towards another, harm them?

They can be conscious of them; they can feel an 'atmosphere'; the perpetrator experiences an unnatural emotion, a seeming feeling of righteousness. When they are thoughts and not words they are surreal. There are those who enjoy being critical. It is when those thoughts are put into words that harm is done. There are those who enjoy a 'good old gossip' and those who enjoy listening and joining in.

What facts do you know, how much is surmise? Would you like your own integrity being discussed? This is a one-sided event, not a conversation.

Where is the love for another being shown in these circumstances?

Do not judge dear ones.

A Child Asks

A child asks, 'who made God?' What is the answer?

God is another word for Good, so God is Good and Good is God. Therefore, who made Good?

Good is the All, the Essence, the Being of everything. You ascend the heavenly staircase, with Good accompanying you all the way, and when you reach the top, what do you find? Why, All Good. You are ever in and of Good. It is in you and all around you. You cannot get away from it. It is the I AM. It was, is and ever will be. You cannot conceive of it being made.

Apply this to Love. You are ever held in Love. It also is in you and all around you. You cannot get away from it. It is Me. It was, is and ever will be. Good and Love are One. You are Good and Love personified. When you reach the Ultimate you will BE, you will BE Good and Love. In other words, you will be Me; you will be part of, yet the whole of, Good and Love.

Do not be afraid to admit to yourselves that you are Good. It is easier, when you use the word 'Good', to say even now, 'I am Good', then one day you will be able to say 'I am God' without feeling arrogance and guilt.

You have been brought up, most of you, to fear God. You were mainly not told you were all good, all love. Jesus was able to say 'I and my Father are ONE'. He was what you call a Master, therefore it was easier for him to say that because he knew it in his very being.

You who use inner thought know you are progressing along a path of Truth. You KNOW the Truth when you hear it. KNOW the Truth and the Truth shall set you free.

You came from Good, you are Good and you will return to Good. You can say 'I came from God and I shall return to God', but it is the bit in the middle that you are AFRAID of – to dare to say 'I am God' is a blasphemy, an unreality, a misnomer. (You think!) But you are happy to know you are part of God and as you and I are One, therefore you CAN dare to say, quietly to yourself, I am God.

Even though I have been reading and learning and doing this work for a long time, I am not comfortable with even thinking about saying 'I am God'. It is unthinkable, it is presumptuous, arrogant. Please help us more over this dear God.

I am the All; I have just told you you are part of Me.

Yes, but if I liken this to my parents, I can say I am their child, but I could not say, 'I am my father or I am my mother'.

But when you meet them again, you will feel that 'belonging', without the 'you and them' feeling. There will be an at-one-ment that is more noticeable than you realised before. And remember, in a past life, they might have been *your children*!

That still doesn't help me to say, 'I am God'. I could more easily listen to Thom Hartmann say, 'I am God' than to the Pope or the Archbishop of Canterbury say that!

For now, keep saying, 'I am Good' for that will make you think! Give you something to live up to!

Over-View

In view of the way mankind is behaving, can You still see us as your perfect children, dear God? When you watch the wars, the terrorism, the murders, the greed, do you still love us without judgment?

Yes, to both those questions. I have said before, you are as little children. Do you hate and judge your own children when they kick the cat or throw a stone through your window? No, you point to the way of thoughtfulness and kindness and you forgive them for 'they know not what they do'. You look for a reason as to why they behave so, or you cause them to think about their behaviour.

Yes, but we also feel very annoyed and frustrated and irritated! We punish too.

If you portray those feelings is it as effective as if you stay calm and try to understand them and see the root cause of their problem?

No. But we are not perfect parents.

But you are my perfect children! You are just forgetting to be so. You have all the tools for being perfect – love, unselfishness, thoughtfulness, patience, time for others, understanding, and this applies not only for your children, but for all people of all nations. These tools are free and cannot harm or hurt. Instead you make and use weapons of destruction against each other. Where is it getting you?

How will it help if I too cause mayhem to punish you? Even more people, innocent people, will suffer. I have an over-view.

You have a wonderful means of showing others how to live happily – your television screens. Instead of violence being used to entertain, and the re-running of war films, how about appealing to your inner good with stories of love and unselfishness, good overcoming seeming evil. You already show amazingly good and true documentaries about insects, animals and children that are appealing to *millions*. The 'happy ever after' instinct is in all of you. That tenderness in your heart centre is easily awakened, appealed to, felt by you.

You all know that you cannot continue as you are now. Your resources are running out as well as your patience. When enough of you, all over the earth plane, stake your claim for Peace, your right to happiness, your conscientious objection to violence of all kinds, heed will be taken by the few because of the many. But many, many, need to make those positive claims, knowing that Good will prevail.

Remember always about Prayer and Right Thought.

Enthusiasm

God, what do you wish me to write about?

You are smiling because your gold rose is dancing about and looking upwards instead of towards you!

How on earth do you know that? It looks a bit silly, hence my smile, but it looks very confident and happy!

It is reflecting your mood. You are making a new decision about publishing our previous book, 'Good God', by a different means. Optimism is a form of positivity. Look back on your past achievements and remember your terrific optimism before the events became a reality. You have forgotten the doubts and fears, as you should do.

I also recall the great enthusiasm of my family and friends prior to each event. And the wonderful practical help from people I hardly knew – builders, solicitor, reps, acquaintances. And their genuine joy at my success. The amazing helpers that were sent to me just when I needed them. There was the odd doubting Thomas who tried to pull me down, but couldn't. And they were rather dull, pessimistic people.

You often recall how a very special friend spoke of your determination and enthusiasm and you said 'may I ever be so'. Then yesterday you wondered if you had been chosen for this present work because of your tenacity.

Do not be modest about these attributes – I gave them to you and you use them like an artist uses his painting abilities or a musician his musical attributes. You all have attributes and it is good for others to see you using them. Do not be backward about coming forward as an example. It encourages others and you never know how much help you may have been.

That is a pleasant way of putting it and makes me feel better about writing your words down. I need many more of your words to help those who are queuing up to get on the spiritual ladder. It is an exciting place to be.

So long as you remember to hold on tightly and not look back or down. Always up. Like your golden rose is now showing you. The diamond in its very centre is now catching the Light and you know not at this moment where it will be reflected back to the earth plane.

What an encouraging thought.

Starvation

I have been asked again, "How can there be a loving God when there are all those starving children in the world?" I should have known by now how to answer, but I didn't. Please help.

The sight of those starving children brings out your compassion more that the sight of dead soldiers. You feel man has asked for trouble with his actions, but that the children are innocent.

I have explained before, you do not know what the past lives of those children have been. Some have chosen to suffer in order to bring out your compassion; others are living now to experience what they have caused in the past.

You mean they are working out their karma?

Few of you can recall past lives; none of you can recall all your past lives. You certainly cannot recall the past lives of others. You can surmise, you can try to imagine, but you have no real knowledge.

Remember this is such a minute part of eternity. You do not understand Time. How long was a bad dream? It may have seemed like hours, when it was but a few seconds. So you will look back on this earth life as a dream, the unreality that it is.

But it can be terrible while it lasts. The pain, the hunger, the heat or cold, the floods or the lack of water is unimaginable to us, even though we feel their suffering in our hearts.

Again I say, when will you learn to share, to love unconditionally, to give generously? Do you think I am causing this situation? You do not like to think of Me as an onlooker, yet I cannot 'interfere' because that takes away your free will.

If these children are paying off karma, does it mean that the poor mothers are also? Did they really choose to suffer like this? Will it make them 'better' people when they can look back from a higher state? Will we then understand why we suffer our ups and downs, our illnesses, our own shortages?

Were things like the Black Death and the Great Plague 'arranged' for the benefit of paying off karma?

You are thinking there are too many souls suffering in comparison with what you believe to be an equivalent number of victims.

You do not realise how many souls have inflicted death and injury over thousands of years. You don't even know off-hand how many casualties were caused by the last two World Wars. Each 'side' is an enemy to the other 'side', even though many are fighting for what they believe to be a right cause.

I have asked you, where is it getting you? You do not anticipate war in heaven any more than you anticipate using money or killing others. And some of you, many of you, do not believe you are going on to another life.

There is NO DEATH, remember? Without experiences how will you experience? When you, or an animal, are never shown love, how do you react to love? You are afraid to be touched. You cannot believe another can truly wish to extend a hand of help and understanding.

Shouting, bullying, quarrelling, go on in your own homes; is it surprising that it goes on in the world? If you cannot live peaceably within your own walls, how can you live peacefully with your neighbours? And how can you live peacefully with your neighbours in other countries?

The love of you dear ones who have learned to care, is so needed. It is hard for you to imagine so much hate and greed. You are thinking this is a sad conversation today. Yes, it is, but you have brought these conditions on yourselves. The Real You is not grasping, selfish, violent. The Real You is not self-satisfied with your behaviour. You bury the Real You in self-righteousness, pride, arrogance. The false you thinks that is something to be proud of and that gentleness and love are weak.

My children, you are learning in such a hard way – and there is no need. You hurt yourselves when you hurt others. You, some of you, have never known the glory of love and giving; the joy of living life in peace and tranquillity; the beauty of scene, music, beautiful music, not the noise some of you call melody!

Would you call this judgment or am I stating facts? And is the answer with Me or you?

Progress & Knowledge

Why is it some people don't want to believe there is something else after death, even though they declare, "I've had enough", meaning life seems no longer worth living?

Would it help if we used some of your analogies? "There are none so blind as those who won't see, none so deaf as those who won't hear". These are people who like to be *right* in all they say and do, even when they are *wrong*. When they think there is no proof about a subject, they do not want to commit themselves. This is a form of fear.

Progress depends much on upbringing and the absorption of your early teaching and learning. Females more readily use their instinct, their intuition; males rely more on their bodily strength and what they consider is their better judgment.

It is noticeable there are more women than men in certain churches and gatherings to do with religion.

All my children have the ability to go deep within. Deep within is all Truth and that is where the right chord is found and struck. It is there in the silence lies all knowledge. It is not the brain in your head that is the 'fountain of all knowledge', that acts as the keyboard for the computer wherein lies the record, the programme.

You can hear just one chord of music and know what melody is coming forth, yet there are those who are tone-deaf. Many of you have strong desires to follow a certain path in life, or a strong leaning towards certain abilities. Others meander along, content to take a day at a time.

When a seed is ready to sprout, it will commence its growth. You can help it along, you can give it moisture and warmth, but if the season is wrong it will wilt. Some seeds push through the earth in a matter of days; others take months, lying dormant before they make progress.

You watch the progress of babies, children at school, youngsters learning a trade, adults tackling a new craft or science; all vary in their speed of progress. You do not know at what stage others are as they journey through this particular incarnation.

All can be helped by love and understanding, by encouragement, but none can be helped by force.

When you crave to learn more about Who You Really Are, you find those around willing and able to help you on your way, and they use only love and patience.

As we have had so many incarnations on this earth plane, why do we mostly seem to be so primitive in our continued fighting and warring?

Mainly because you use your free will selfishly. You still prefer to take than to give. You continue to want what is not yours. You do not like self-discipline and you no longer teach your children self-discipline and you are experiencing the result. If you fail to train your dog to behave it becomes a nuisance to its owners and everyone around. When you do not restrain your desire for unhealthy food, for drugs, for over indulgence of any kind, you suffer the results.

You are punishing yourselves.

But why don't we do more about it?

Quite simply, because you don't want to.

But surely you can 'arrange' to send us more souls to show us a better way.

I have, but you don't listen to them! You think you are enjoying your bad dream. You think the nightmare is preferable to a state of Heaven on Earth.

But what about those of us who look on and dislike what we see?

You are the fortunate ones! You have found the path that leads to contentment and contentment contains your heaven – you want for nothing, neither do you wish for more. Your feast can be a simple meal that tastes wonderful and costs little, but those who are satisfied only when they are spending more than they have at the most expensive venues feel sorry for you, if they stop to think about you.

I keep recalling the saying, "the meek shall inherit the earth". Where does that come in?

Do you remember we talked about you not owning your piece of earth, that it is rented to you, free? Therefore you cannot inherit land in that sense, but you can inhabit it and the time will come when "the meek will inhabit the earth".

It will be a time of Peace and Love and it WILL come. Meek need not mean timid and docile. It can mean thoughtful and caring.

You all know people who are thoughtful and caring, unselfish, yet strong in their convictions for good. Every time you pray for Peace and Light you are adding weight to the scales for Good and Love to manifest.

Rise above the turmoil and look down on an earth plane of peace and plenty. It IS happening and each one of you has the power to help it to happen.

Complete Trust

My mind seems to be a complete blank as regards what I am to write about. Sometimes I get really helpful messages when I am in this state. Please use me, dear God.

Your former pink rose bud will not stay in your mental picture frame. It keeps being replaced by the recent yellow rose, upright and fully open with red tipped petals. And what is happening to those petals?

They are blowing off in a breeze in all directions, gradually leaving only the stamens behind.

And you are afraid to interpret this symbol in the way that comes to your mind. Why?

Because it could be my mortal mind's interpretation and I am afraid to read this, afraid of getting my dream shattered by too much optimism.

And what are the two things that we so often talk about as being opposites to each other?

Love and Fear.

Exactly. Fear shuts out Love and Love knows no Fear.

You are spending your waking hours wishing for our book, 'Good God', to be widely published. You are afraid of disappointment, afraid to be too optimistic. Do you not realise that those thoughts put a barrier in the way of progress? There have been many, many occasions when you have pictured that book going out and out and out all over the world. You have 'seen' it, you have made a reality of it. Why spoil that picture now, just when, deep down, you are full of hope?

You know that every page of that book can help someone, somewhere. That it opens just at the right page for the moment, as do some of your other books. *I* do not wish to prevent that happening, so who does?

No one that I know of. I am not normally afraid of optimism nor normally given to pessimism.

When you mentally hold that book and a possible publisher and the business side of the transaction in the Light, step into that Light yourself. Without you none of this would have happened.

When you pray for a loved one or a friend who is going to have an operation, you do not only hold that person in the Light, you include the surgeon and the nurses. The surgeon is vital to the outcome – along with the prayers of others. Even when you hold in the Light beautiful flowers that have been given to you, you include the giver. When you put the protection of the Light over those who travel to dangerous zones, you include the vehicle in which they are travelling.

So complete your 'picture'. The day *will* come when the petals blow in all directions! I remind you again, we do not waste our resources.

When you say 'we', do you mean those who, on a higher plane, work for the furtherance of your guidance, your Good?

What do you imagine all the souls on the next plane are doing? You know they do not stand around, doing nothing. We have talked about this before. You have read about this. You choose your 'job', just as you choose your work on the earth plane. You choose to work for pleasure and help. You do not get 'baby-sitters' to stand in for you while you attend to something else.

Your children would become better citizens if parents chose to give more of their time to them on earth, instead of handing them over to others while they pursued other means of work or entertainment.

Do you think your guides and teachers on this side forget to care for you, hand you over to someone who does not know you so well? And you forget that *I* am always with you under all circumstances. I know your every thought, your every need, your every move. Recall about putting items in my In Tray, then leaving Me to deal with them. There is no great pile, where some items get forgotten. Remember all is movement.

At all times work with right motives, unselfishness, caring, thought for others. As with all that is good, all comes back to you, pushed down and running over.

Trust Me.

Dreams & Dreaming

Why are you not delving into what you are thinking, and asking Me questions?

Because it all seems rather futile. I am using my little mind, not my Higher Mind. I am re-dreaming in my waking state the dreams I had last night in my sleep state. I dream so much lately, such real scenes, wonderful colours, possible scenarios. Yet when I awake they do not matter; they have been of no consequence.

They do not matter; they are not matter.

And you are going to tell me this life is all a dream? But does it matter?

In the realms of eternity do your present thoughts matter? Will it matter next week, next month, next year what you are thinking now?

No, not while I am re-living last night's dreams, but suppose I was deciding that I would plant a new hedge, or move house, or buy a new car – that would make a difference to next week, next month, next year. The hedge would have grown, I would be living in a different place and riding in a different vehicle – that would all be different. I would be seeing and doing different things.

Those may be trivial events, but suppose I had never lived in West Africa, borne children, married, created gardens, I would then be a different person, different in outlook, without those experiences.

When man designs an enormous engine with thousands of parts, he already knows how each part will work and what it is for. He may use up a whole incarnation to perfect that engine. Then other men use that engine, often giving no thought to its original creator. Some make adjustments; some rip it to pieces, some nurture it. The original engine has changed, yet it was created by Thought and remains in Thought.

You, all of you, were created in Thought, since when you have changed shape, changed colour, moved around, but the original Thought remains intact.

I cannot connect this with dreaming. If I dig and plant a bare piece of land with shrubs and grass and flowers and vegetables, it will not be the same piece of land – or will it? I will have envisioned the end result and others will come along and alter it, but the original piece of land remains the same. I have just altered the look of it. So it would seem that however we live, we go back to our original 'spark' of the Whole? Has the moving around, the living many times, not altered our original Self, therefore it has just been an experience?

Am I now beginning to understand that you, God, needed to experience yourself through being us? This is what I have been reading about and finding difficult to understand.

Yes, my child. What you thought was going to be rather a useless conversation has become profound. You are grasping the dream. You are seeing beyond and before and ahead of the dream. For a few moments of your time you returned 'home'.

I need to think about this. While I am tuned-in I can begin to understand, but will I comprehend this tomorrow and next week?

The Meaning of Love

It doesn't feel right when I am not tuning-in to you dear God, Good. There is a restlessness, a feeling of laziness, a wasting of precious time. Please use me.

You have been a long way with your thoughts since you wrote that sentence.

You have travelled along many roads of what you think are different kinds of Love. You have recalled long, long ago when White Eagle was your grandfather and Minesta was your beloved mother. Then you felt disloyalty to your parents of this life. Why? Love is whole, it is beautiful. You do not feel guilty for loving your sons equally in this life. Would you not feel great guilt if you loved one more than the other? You can experience different aspects of Love, but that does not detract from Love itself.

Think of a beautiful diamond, scintillating in a bright light. You see many colours; all are wondrous; all are different; all are part of the whole diamond.

Picture a great tree in Springtime; new buds burst forth; you marvel at the strength and colour being displayed; it fills you with hope of things to come. Then you see it in full leaf, changing with the early morning light through to sunset, casting shadows, shade, peace. Then its leaves turn colour in Autumn and you marvel again at the display of Nature. Then is appears to sleep through the cold months. But the same great tree is there – solid, reliable, whole.

Love is everywhere, free for all to experience. It surrounds all of you at all times. You 'feel good' when you experience it, when you give it out and when you receive it. You can pour Love into everything – people, animals, plants, even inanimate things, and it re-arranges their 'atoms' even though you have not yet learned to recognise this.

Love is so powerful some of my children are afraid of it! So that says they are afraid of Good, for Good is Love and Love is Good. Then remember God is Good and God is Love and Love is God, all Good. And you are all Good, all Love, therefore you are God.

We had this conversation recently, when I said I cannot say 'I am God'. It is a monstrous statement.

And I said, 'Say I am Good if that makes you feel better!'

You were reading yesterday about God, Me, having to experience myself and how do I do that? By becoming You and You and You, so there you have your answer.

Count Your Blessings

I want to forget my aches and pains, my tiredness and slight depression. Please cheer me up, dear God.

"Count your blessings one by one"

Yes, I know that quote and I DO count my blessings, you know that God.

You are letting the state of the Nations get to you. Know that you are helping those people and conditions with your prayers and affirmations. You are one of thousands doing the same. Your thoughts do have an effect and without the Good that people of all nations and races are doing and thinking, conditions would be much worse.

Surely they could not be much worse? Millions are homeless, starving, sick, without any possessions. Without hope.

You are thinking that great earthquakes that wiped them off the planet would be a blessing.

Yes, for they would then be better off, back 'home' from where they came.

And from where did they come? You do not all come from nor return to a place of perfect peace. You earn your environments, your experiences.

But You do not punish us; you forgive us; you love us.

I forgive you and I love you, but you punish yourselves. Your conscience guides you, moves you around, teaches you. It is so easy to use and experience your conscience. A small child soon learns that fire burns and hurts, that water can be too deep or too cold. Animals and birds know their limitations.

So there is hell. We make our own hell?

Hell is a name for discomfort. Hell is not a place; it is a condition.

So is heaven not a place but a condition?

You, many of you, know that you can experience heaven on earth and you are looking on at those experiencing hell on earth.

But there are babies suffering in the circumstances of which I speak!

You came to this earth as a baby, but you did not leave your previous life as a baby. You chose to return to experience. Every soul on your earth plane is experiencing an experience! In all eternity it is but a brief encounter.

Do we have to experience misery, murder, starvation as well as beauty, love and peace?

How can you help another's pain, another's loss' another's exaltation if you have not experienced it yourself?

Isn't it a hard way to live! So few are extremely happy; even those with everything they could wish for rarely seem satisfied.

Doesn't that speak for itself? It is not the material things that matter. You know that. It is the love for one another, the kindness, the unselfishness, the thoughtfulness that makes you happy, even elated.

You do not know what is in another's mind. Would you change places with anyone you know, or know of?

No. Not anyone.

Then why are you somewhat sad and depressed? In some ways the rich and especially the powerful need your prayers as much as the deprived and the sick.   "Count your blessings"!

Frustration

It is eighteen months since I had your book printed, dear God. You said several times your messages were not just for me. Why do I not find a suitable publisher? Why are the printed copies moving so slowly in some districts?

You are not expecting any helpful answers, are you?

No. I am sorry if that is being negative. I cannot help being disappointed because as I re-read all you have said in "Good God" it is so much easier to understand and accept than in many other books, therefore very appealing to those who are newly seeking your Truth.

As you type this you can hear that tractor ploughing the enormous field behind your home. You are not expecting that work to be done quickly. The tractor is moving fast, but it has hundreds of furrows to plough.

Seed was sown many months ago – tiny seeds that required planting into the soil – there to lie dormant for a time, before pushing through the earth into the light. When that happened, sunlight and rain poured down to enable those seeds to become plants, growing slowly to reach maturity. They became food and much work still required doing to get that food gathered and prepared for distribution – distribution to the right places for the right people at the appropriate time.

You watched those seeds being sown, you watched them grow into plants, you saw them being harvested, but you have no idea where they have gone, except you know they are somewhere in what you call 'the food chain'.

I understand this analogy, but that farmer knew how to contact a suitable distributor and the distributor knew where to take the corn. I planted the seed you gave me; it grew enough for a book. You guided me to a printer. Then I became a very small distributor, but not big enough for the job. Please, please guide me to a publisher so that this end product can spread as it needs to, to feed those who are hungry for this kind of food.

Do you remember your mother once saying to you, "stick it old girl – don't give up now"?

Oh, how well I remember that moment. It makes her feel very near me; I am experiencing similar tears of frustration.

I will not give up this assignment.

Thinking & Feeling

I am not tuning-in to write this section. It is me, Betty, again communicating direct with you, my reader.

How are you doing? Is what you have been reading making sense to you? Are you progressing and realising that we are ALL part of GOOD and that God is not a person?

We are thinking and feeling at all times. Prove it now by trying not to! Even if you think you have made your mind a blank, chances are you are noticing a crooked picture on the wall or a piece of fluff on the carpet. Even if you shut your eyes you are remembering you left the gate open or forgot to order more fuel. Perhaps you are noticing your leg aches or your back itches. You see you are thinking and feeling.

Your brain is your box of tools, your dictionary, your reference book, your vast copy of instructions for every item you use. It is a priceless possession, but it does not have feelings.

So now I want you to 'think in your heart centre' where all real feeling is. If you nearly drop something, where does your free hand go? Why, to your chest, (or to your solar plexus) not to your head. If you suffer a loss, or experience great joy, where do you feel it? Why, in your heart centre.

For those of you who do not understand about your chakras, I would explain that they are places of entry into your material body from your etheric body. (If you can accept it, from your Soul Body). I will describe just three of these chakras as I understand them. There is one on the crown of your head where knowledge pours in; one at your heart centre where Love pours in and one at your solar plexus where there is feeling.

You can begin to see why it is so important what you 'let in' to your chakras. They are as wonderful as your sight and your hearing. They are great centres of sensitivity and they require intelligent use. If someone is 'draining' you with their worries and troubles, hold your hands across your solar plexus.

Think of some of our sayings and you begin to understand where they came from. "My heart goes out to her", "I feel for him", "my heart aches" – very different from a headache.

Do you begin to feel how we are all attached? We are all different yet all the same, all part of the Whole. And you need to apply that to Nature. We are part of it. Love your pet; pick it up, stroke it, and you 'feel' something. Look at a flower, inhale its perfume, and you 'feel' something. Lean against a great tree and absorb its strength. This is not airy fairy stuff. It is real and you can luxuriate in it.

Picture a great hall full of people, all there to hear another speak. It makes no difference what their colour nor their creed, they hope to absorb something into themselves – through their head chakra, and their heart chakra will sort out its Truth or otherwise. Come to think of it, our Conscience must be in our heart centre and not our head, for our brain would not know right from wrong; it would not be able to sort out that one. Here I think it is our 'Higher Mind' that we listen to, the one that we are using to read this. Our Higher Mind is the Mind of God – our Mind of Good.

Now accept that there are many ways of displaying Truth, of showing Feeling, of controlling Thought. We must not expect everyone to be exactly like us, but what is so important is to be open to fresh, different, new thoughts. If we 'knew it all' we would be perfect and if we think we 'know it all' we are pretty unbearable. If you look back, how much have you changed over the years? Why are you reading this? Would you have been doing so twenty, forty, sixty years ago?

It is so important to be open to change. How did we learn to *do* or *think*? Something or someone taught us. Where did they learn? Suddenly a new book or a different person shows us an alternative and we wonder why we never thought of it ourselves because it is so much easier or so much clearer.

And that of course brings me to this different understanding of God.

We are taught that God is All Love – ALL LOVE – yet we are also told that we will be punished if we do not do His Will. What is His Will? He has given us Free Will so it would be very unkind to punish us for using it, and All Love doesn't know how to punish, for punishment hurts and Love never hurts. The lack of it does. We keep punishing ourselves – we have done it for thousands of years. Aren't we slow to learn and to change?

We are now told we must not touch children in school. We know why, but aren't we sowing more seeds of fear and displaying a lack of *feeling*? Small children need a cuddle when they are sad or hurt. What thoughts and feelings are we implanting? By all means tell children there are sometimes 'sick' people about who might want to harm them, to be careful who touches them and where and when. And to tell an adult straight away if they are worried. Children have a very strong instinct about right and wrong. Its use should be encouraged at all ages.

I can remember, when I was about seven, being allowed to go for rides in the car belonging to the husband of some old family friends. I was thrilled because he let me sit in the passenger seat and help steer and sound the horn. What I didn't like, and what seemed very odd, was that he put his free hand on my bare thigh. Instinct was very strong in me on those few occasions. I didn't query why to myself, I just 'instinctively knew it wasn't right'. I didn't mention it to my parents – *instinct* must have told me they might have stopped the rides!

Let us absorb as much as we can from these messages I am privileged to receive from Good. I like to remember the one that told how our prayers are 'gathered up and added to all the others, causing a great Light to shine back upon the earth, bringing and spreading Peace and Love". We forget that we can be very Powerful for Good. We forget to remember why we are here and Who We Wish to BE and Who We Really Are.

Sometimes is seems easier to feel 'down' than 'up', but when we are 'up' we wonder why we ever allow ourselves to be 'down'!

We are never alone, we can always 'tune in' to Good, we are guided but never forced, we are Perfect in God, Good, and our ultimate goal is to experience perfection. It is up to us to attain that. Let us use our tools more efficiently and certainly more lovingly.

Taking a Rest

God, what am I supposed to be doing?

The yellow rose is sitting on a wall with its head on its hand; it doesn't know which way to jump. You wish you could draw this picture.

You are going through a testing time. You do not like having to wait and see. You know you haven't lost your way – you just can't see ahead and you don't like to be in that position.

I tell you, all of you, it is good to have to halt at times. Your feelings of patience, trust, even knowing, are all being put to the test. Answer your own questions as they come to your mind. You can do this.

Say to yourself, "I believe that I have done the best I can with my present knowledge and understanding. I know that I must now entrust others to use their knowledge. Certain things are not in my hands just now."

Trust Me to take the weight. Remember you are entitled to time off. Your body and your mind can have a rest. Your Mind never rests, not even when you sleep.

All WILL be well. All IS well now.

74

Body, Mind & Spirit

Dear God, several 'orthodox' religions have been shown recently on our television screens. I can't understand how human beings are so far from your simple Truth about Who We Really Are and Who You Really Are.

I can only describe some of their rituals as antics, and laughable at that. Now if that offends them, I hasten to include our Western religious rituals – wearing certain gowns and crowns and rings, chanting, using a 'different' voice from normal, and so on.

Great Masters of the past surely did not demand all this? Jesus preached from many places, both inside and out, wearing just a plain long raiment, as portrayed in all the paintings we see. Did he ever tell us what to wear or how to move?

Jesus came to you as an example. He talked to you, he did not command. He showed you how best to live and behave; how to interact with your brothers and sisters. His words were so simple. His teaching was all Love and all about Love. Love one another. Be as little children.

You have added so much to the simple Truth that it has become like stripping off layers and layers of paint to get to the original woodwork. You cease doing some things, but continue with others, even adding to them. You apply rules and regulations not only to what you wear, but to what you eat, how you move, when you should pray, even your phraseology.

You are already my perfect children, all made of flesh and blood and bone structure and with a brain. That is your body. You have a Mind which works on various levels. Then you are Spirit – not a spirit. You are therefore Body, Mind & Spirit. Some of you are grasping this and putting it into practice and writing about it.

Spirit is all around you and IN you. Life is all around you and IN you. Thought is all around you and IN you. You have the ability to use your Mind and your Body because you are ever guided and held in Spirit. Spirit is Me, whom you call God, but I am not a person. I am experiencing Myself through you.

Now you can understand that I have some extraordinary experiences! I have to dress up for myself, bow down to myself, even fear myself – because you, trying to be Me, are doing all these things. As parents, do you make your children wear certain clothes to speak to you? Do they have to use a special voice to speak to you? Do they have to lie on the floor or climb a tree to get your attention? Well, yes sometimes, because you do not give them your full attention!

But you always have my full attention and I already know all that you are thinking, scheming, hoping, feeling. We are never apart, so why do you try to get more attention with your bodies and your voices? All is Peace and Love and the quieter you are, the calmer you are, the nearer you come to being Who You Really Are, which is part of Me. You go to a place of tranquillity and silence to find perfect Peace. Where is perfect peace when you are having to concentrate on your lower mind and your body?

How can it help you to get nearer to me because you are using ritual?

Do you think you are more likely to 'go to heaven' because you have repeated certain words or performed certain actions? You never DIE so you must be going somewhere! If you are full of fear at the time of your death it may take a little longer for you to 'wake up', but wake up you will.

And where do you find yourself? Exactly where you expected to find yourself! If you thought there was nothing after your earthly life, you will wake up to something very similar – a dreamlike state, similar to that which you have left, except you will experience no pain, a 'nothingness' that will make you want to move on. It is then that you will realise you are still alive, that you are not alone.

If you have already envisaged your next 'home', you will experience the 'house and garden' you have imagined – it will become your reality. If you have already chosen those you most wish to meet on your arrival, joy of joys, they will be there to welcome you!

Why do you fill your earth life with so many fears? What is there to fear? It is yourself that you fear – coming face to face with yourself as you know yourself. Only you and I know your real self and I do not punish, remember? So you must be fearing your own punishment. Doesn't that make you wish to change your ways, your thoughts, your outlook, so that you can Love Yourself?

Food for thought, is it not?

Soul

12.10.04

Yesterday's dialogue about Body, Mind & Spirit particularly appealed to me and I have already read it several times. There is one item that is not mentioned; where does Soul come in?

You have already thought about this during the morning and now you are concerned that you will be adding your thoughts instead of Mine. You still do not realise that so much of what you say to yourself is already Me answering you.

Well, when I haven't tuned-in to You, it can be just the little me having a conversation with myself! I could be 'making it all up' just to suit how the little me feels.

And your 'little me' is so often now being entirely in agreement with your Higher self. You connect with Me a great deal of your thinking day. You and I are one, remember? Do you realise you rarely need to picture your rose now when you use Me. You open the book without stopping to look at the cover. You turn to the new blank page, ready to work on this level.

As usual you are right! I do rarely use my rose, neither the previous pink rosebud nor the current golden rose. And whereas in the past the rose was static, now it portrays something to me in its position or movements. As I physically look at the Peace rose on my desk at this moment it brings me complete stillness and calm.

So now we will continue to talk about Soul. You, all of you, are Spirit and your Soul is your individualized Spirit. You are all the same, yet all different. In your sameness you are all different. How else would you recognise one another? Even identical twins are not! Your Soul recognises it is part of Spirit for it is *en rapport* with its Source.

You can be in a great Hall of people all listening to a wonderful Speaker, or to a beautiful Concert, or to a famous Singer; you are all spellbound, euphoric, perhaps perfectly still, but each one of you is absorbing a different note or word or sound. It is not striking the same chord in each Soul. That is why when you read a deep book you absorb different parts of it at that particular moment in time. The emphasis can move from word to word or note to note according to your particular desire or need at that moment.

You, yourself, have realised that all people do not see the same colour when looking at the same flower or piece of silk. You know this has nothing to do with colour blindness. You have been taught to call that colour red or blue or green, but you have no way of knowing what your partner is seeing. Putting a matching colour with it still does not prove you see the same.

This brings me to asking you again, are there soul mates?

You are All soul mates.

Oh no, I am not a soul mate with that man or woman who is thrashing their child, nor that person who is decrying You in every aspect.

You are All One. You are all part of the Whole. You are all connected. You are all part of me. A litter of puppies is a litter of puppies even though one is brown, one black and one a mixture of both. They all came from the same source. We are back to them being individualized, by appearance and character; colour and breed. Now you can see how this applies to human beings.

And I like to think those puppies are all part of Spirit, each with a little Soul. And I believe and hope we shall find our pets in the next world.

Why not? Why should any of my Creation stay earthbound? And you will love other breeds equally, just as you will love other individual Souls equally, because you will realise they are all part of the Whole.

If you had been living in a grey, dirty city all your life, never having travelled any distance away from it, wouldn't it be a revelation of delight to witness fields and mountains and rivers; flowers and wild animals. That happened to evacuees in wartime Britain. That is what is going to happen to you when you behold the 'heaven world' of which you now only dream. You will awake from your present dream when your wake-up call comes, and believe Me when I tell you your ecstasy will be beyond your present comprehension.

Do not cling on to those who are ready to depart the earth plane for you are keeping them from paradise.

Angels

God, there is so much written about angels and they are still portrayed with wings. I find myself putting them in the same category as cupid, and sitting on a cloud with a harp!

Am I right in thinking 'angel' is a word which applies to beautiful souls who spend their time on higher planes, sending out and down wonderful help to us when we most need it; that they are Beings who can come very close to us, guiding us with their superior knowledge? That they do not need crystals and other symbols to bring them close?

Man feels a need to portray his inner feelings in words, song, poetry and painting. He needs to go beyond the earthly visual seeing and hearing because that does not satisfy his innermost. He therefore conjures up something that better satisfies his need.

To show some people to be above others he has devised different images. Materially, he puts crowns on kings and queens, robes and symbols on clergy, medals on the heroic. Spiritually, he adds wings, lights, halos, even trumpets to portray higher beings.

You could say, 'if it helps do it, if it doesn't forget it'.

Those of you who can use your psychic sense can see the Light around each one of you. You are in and of that Light. The real you is not flesh and blood, it is Spirit.

You have put great value on gold and diamonds. Yes, they are beautiful, but you might have chosen tin and malachite.

This is all part of your striving to reach out and up to the Higher State that, instinctively, you know is there.

Your Soul remembers its higher state. Mortal mind is trying to reach your soul just as your soul longs to return to its origin, which is Spirit.

I have told you, you are never alone. You have guides and teachers around you and many of you are conscious of these; then you have Higher Beings who have advanced beyond your ken who come close to you in times of great need.

Let Me give you a simile. Let us use Higher Education as an example. Lecturers and Professors are teaching you advanced subjects because you are anxious to learn more. Sometimes one of you asks a very difficult question or has great difficulty grasping a fact. A more highly advanced teacher is required by your present don and he seeks the advice of his superior – someone who knows more. He or she will not be wearing wings, but he or she is there when more information is needed.

You revere that higher authority. In your heart you may bow down to them, but you do not get up and bow to them. You thank them. They are there to help you. And in the heaven world as you call it, they do it with great love and understanding.

Do you begin to understand who Angels are?

Cause & Effect (ii)

I have been asked if you will enlarge on a point you made recently. I said I was not a soul mate of the parent who thrashed its child and you said, "You are all One, you are all connected, all part of Me".

We will start with the child. It experienced pain, fear, injustice, maybe hate. As it developed it may have used and passed on those traits, it certainly felt them and was affected by them. But it may have been given the opportunity of reversing those hurtful ways, caused by the love and example of another soul. It may have developed a far greater love and compassion than a lesser affected soul. And as its love grew it was able to forgive its aggressor, so it advanced greatly.

As to the aggressor; here you have either an undeveloped soul or a revengeful soul. It experienced power over another, 'getting its own back' from a past hurt, nothing to do with its child. It was trying to regain its self worth. But instead of progressing it degenerated; it lost all that was worthwhile. It may have stayed in that state for a whole incarnation, only experiencing itself after its death – its re-entry to its source. Alternatively, circumstances might have been presented to it that filled it with remorse – remorse so great it was almost unbearable.

Can you now feel compassion for both these souls, for your wrong judgment can only add fuel to fire? Your love and understanding can 'help them on their way'.

Apply this to wars. Each side feels 'right', justified, angry. Those in power feel entitled to give orders to fight, usually for what is not theirs. The atmosphere in war zones is horrific; it is stifling, furious, mighty. Men have been trained to obey, so they kill and maim with impunity. But what is it doing to those who are acting against their better judgment, who know it is wrong? They are the few against the many and it affects their Being. These are the men, and women, who require after-help from your psychiatrists and counsellors.

When you go deep within, you cannot disconnect yourselves from these souls. You do not know why they behave so and you do not know that you have not been likewise in the past. This is why you cannot judge and why you *are* all one.

You mentioned an undeveloped soul. As we live for ever and experience hundreds of incarnations, both on this earth plane and other planets, how can we be undeveloped?

If you were fully developed you would no longer be incarnating at this level. There are those who believe, falsely, that you reincarnate as a fish or a bird or an animal. Now reverse that. An amoeba is a single cell, experiencing itself as that. Then it desires to grow. And it does, on and on and on. Plant life experiences itself, on and on and on, often with your help. Do you sometimes wonder if your pet would like to experience itself as you? All is movement, remember? Do you recall in your meditations the great pillars of amethyst, emerald, ruby and other jewels? You have much to learn and to remember my children.

An undeveloped soul is not necessarily an aggressive soul surely?

No, of course not. It is usually a developing soul. But it can be what you might call an 'obstinate' soul which is taking a long time to 'come to its senses' in that it does not grasp the better way of progressing. You can liken so much of what I tell you to your concept of the world and the people around you. All are the same, yet all are different.

If you consider all there is to learn about in your world, let alone the universe around you, how can you possibly study it all in one lifetime?

That takes me back to my belief that it would be better to teach our children more of what really interests them than to try to teach them a little about so much. According to what they want to do with their lives, they have different needs. They will do better if able to choose their subjects. Also, we pick up so much along our various paths through life. What good did it do me to be made to learn Greek?

None at all! The way you have lived your life and the circumstances you have experienced, needed the subjects which you would have chosen!

They were the subjects I put my mind to, namely English grammar and composition, simple mathematics, cookery and handcrafts. All else was a struggle. Travel has improved my geography and history, and television is widening my general knowledge. How much damage is television doing to our children?

You can assess this for yourselves. Watch programmes through *their* eyes and you will see the errors. What are they shown of peace and love, beauty and selflessness? How much emphasis is put on respect, both for their parents and for others? Are they shown how to be helpful and caring? What are they told about Me?

How sad, very little.

Worse & Worse

God, where is improvement? Today, the 19th October 2004, it seems almost certain that our troops in Iraq will be sent into a more dangerous zone, and conditions in Iraq generally are as bad or worse than ever.

Our Government is going to allow the building of great gambling casinos with less restriction on the amount of 'winnings'. More alcohol can be brought into the country without fear of having our cars confiscated!

Where is common sense?

Are there more people in favour of all this licence than against it? Do the public in general think it will make our country a better place? Am I being 'old fashioned'?

First, war is never a solution, but it is taking my people so long to believe that disagreements can be settled by prayer, thought and love. You continue to believe those three tools are less effective than guns, bombs and force.

Again I say, you continue to be dissatisfied with 'your lot'. Looking around, are the people you know, who are trying to make an impression with their wealth, as happy and contented as those of you who treasure your real friends and your lesser possessions? An African can be happy in his mud hut so long as he has his family around and the means of growing food – and no fear of war. You have seen that with your eyes, and *you* felt no fear amongst them, only interest.

You are thinking of the starving Africans; their famine, their floods, their disease. Think deeper, child; think of what has caused much of this. White man still feels superior, but is he? How much is he truly helping them?

As to your new laws about gambling and alcohol – who will gain? The few or the many? Does money have to be the means of making my people happy? You are surrounded by Life – Life in everything, but only man values money, uses money, depends on money.

You are recalling that series of programmes on your television about the trial life on the Isle of Taransay.

Yes. Some participants enjoyed it, a few hated it. I found it enlightening and feasible.

I have said before, and I shall say it again, do not be despondent. More good is being done, said and lived than you realise. It creeps about quietly, but it is putting down roots, strong roots, that will eventually withstand the current turmoil.

Those of you who are strong in Spirit will withstand the trauma and you are, and will be, examples to those who are frightened. By Love and Example you can improve all things for all peoples and all ages. Some 'tough' yet exemplary little people are descending to your earth plane and there will be change, change for the better. Continue to hope and pray and be not afraid to show love in all that you do.

Bless you, my beloved children.

Our Heaven World

For those of us who are not caught up in conflict, how good it is to take each day as it comes, even accepting altered plans when they occur. Just to BE and to absorb what is around us, be it a comfortable home, a beautiful garden or a glorious view. Each leaf, every cloud formation, every sound is different. We miss so much beauty by rushing about.

A friend's budgerigar perched on my hand yesterday, so trusting, so perfect, so magic in its tiny frame. I kept bringing it close to my face and we had an eye-to-eye rapport; I felt those fine gold strands that attach us to all life.

Is this what the heaven world will be like, God? And how will it appeal to those who now seem to thrive on noise and clatter and clutter – all that is un-peaceful? Is anyone, can anyone be bored in heaven, God?

You have forgotten that your next phase is so varied. There are cities as well as gardens and woodland, great vistas and lakes. You are drawn to what appeals to you, to what you remember and those you knew and now remember.

You will 'drop off' much of the dross of this earth plane. You will cease to *want*, and your *needs* will be met. You *will* Wake Up from your present dream. Your nightmares, your illness, your pain, will have remained with your discarded body. Your new raiment will be so light, both in weight and luminosity.

You have been there before; you have been here before. You are always ALIVE! Change 'alive' to 'I live' and 'all live'. Try to imagine feeling completely satisfied, wanting nothing, needing nothing, experiencing joy, fulfilment, completeness. And FREEDOM. Freedom from Fear, fear of anything unpleasant. All this is beyond your present comprehension.

Will you help your earth plane by realising all this could be yours now. All that matters is free now. If and when you live in LOVE you will do nothing but help your fellow men, all creatures, all nature. You will experience Love which is Good which is ME.

Pray for this to materialise. Pray for the Light of Peace to descend upon you and all the earth. It is there now, but you do not believe it. Use it, live in it, absorb it.

Food for Thought

22.10.04

Please tell us about keeping these little babies alive artificially, even when their quality of life is so poor.

Souls are passing backwards and forwards between 'heaven' and earth every moment of the day and night. That is something you forget to remember.

There is no barrier. You on earth try to put one there. This applies to birth and so-called death. You cling on because you are afraid of a nothingness, a loss.

The medical profession feels a need, an obligation, to keep you alive at all times. It can be what they feel is an achievement. Then there are times when they know death would be kinder.

Human parents, especially mothers, long to hold on to that defective child and their love refuses to see that it could be far better to let go, to let 'nature' take its course. In the animal world the female concentrates on her fit offspring, ignoring the runt or the sickly fledgling, often pushing it out of the nest.

Why?

Because she senses that tiny one is not going to develop as it should and her efforts are required by the rest of the brood. Her instinct tells her it is better to discard the imperfect.

But how can that apply to humans?

Humans show more compassion in that they make every effort to nurture their babies, but sometimes they do not think ahead, asking themselves how will the future be. I am not speaking of natural care, oh no. I am referring to artificial means which try to force that life to live on regardless.

84

Whether at birth or death, is it kind to cause another human being to suffer – whether it be a long life ahead or the prolonging of a finishing life?

I can see a lot of free choice here. There is choice by the mother, the doctor, or a relative or friend in the case of the elderly, but what about the free choice of the sufferer, be it the baby or the adult?

You are wondering about the fact that you 'die' when you are destined to die, and, on the other hand, the fact that your life and conditions are being decided by another.

You are also thinking about the law of karma. Think deeply here. You *choose* to return to the earth plane for karmic reasons and this applies to parents and child, to adult and adult. If you choose to use only Love in these cases, the outcome will be right for all concerned, for there are lessons being learned in each situation.

So if it were me having to make up my mind about my deformed baby's future and I chose to let it die, I could be allowing it a better life and perhaps freeing myself as well as my baby from a karmic situation?

Its death would not be in your hands even so, but you could be learning an important lesson about love and selflessness. This is a very deep subject. Remember there is no Chance nor Coincidence, but you are being given the opportunity you asked for. Yes, asked for. When you chose this reincarnation you knew 'what you were in for', yet some of you cannot accept that fact. You say, "Oh no, I would never have chosen to go through all that suffering".

Do you begin to understand how your suffering can help you to develop into Who You Really Are? To become Who You Wish to Be? Look what Jesus chose to go through and what an example that has been to the whole world. The difficulties in life make you strong. They 'bring out the best' in you. You become an example.

What about those who do not cope with their difficulties?

Then they get another opportunity, another incarnation, similar yet different.

Certainly food for thought!

The Armour of Love

God, what is there that really 'gets' to people and makes them think? I mean worthwhile thoughts, not all the rubbish that fills minds and homes and entertainment programmes?

Rarely is it the bright side of life; it is when loss or tragedy hits, either personal or worldwide. Then the little mind queries what life is all about.

While you sail on a calm sea, all you see is water. You do not think about the wonders deep down in that water, nor the beauty above the clouds where the sun always shines.

In other words, most people don't want to think deeply. Of what are they afraid?

Afraid of what they think is the unknown. Causes you to smile, doesn't it? They have been here on earth so many times and passed on so many times.

You'd think they would be used to it by now!

They don't want to remember. Here is where they recall hearing about death and destruction, retribution, lost souls, ghosts, perhaps hell – all that is negative. I and you and many others are trying to help them to 'wake up', but you know how you can take a horse to water but cannot make it drink.

Can't You splash them a bit?

I do. Sometimes they heed; sometimes they don't even feel it; sometimes they wipe it away. Sometimes a sheep leaves the flock, but it is never lost and may have found greener grass. You can live happily on that calm water, asking for little else. But when a storm comes you need shelter, company, assurance that you will be safe, come through it. An experience of any kind leaves its mark, alters your outlook, makes you think.

Sometimes it leaves a great fear.

Then you can be helped by talking to others, confessing your fear, acknowledging it. That can be the commencement of higher thought, of experiencing care from another, a stirring of love, a hope, then a knowing that all is not on the surface as you had thought.

Once you have learned to balance on a bicycle you soon ride on, going faster and faster and enjoying the sensation. So with Truth and Life and Joy. Once you realise it is really there for ever, you can't get enough of it. You keep finding it. It comes to you; you come face to face with it and you wonder why you didn't see it before. Like attracts like. You find new vistas.

Your values change. Suddenly 'the best things in Life are Free'. Fear is dropping away. Life is with you and in you and around you. You are encased in the armour of Love.

A View Beyond

God, I don't really have to tell you that I gain great joy from driving and gardening, because you already know my every thought.

I know there will be no driving on the next plane because we shall not need that mode of travel. Apparently flowers do not wilt and die so there will be no gardening. Presumably we shall eat no vegetables and little fruit.

My other joy would be ballroom dancing, but a friend thinks that is too frivolous to ask you about!

To me, and to two of my friends, ballroom dancing is fantastic, especially with a good partner. Moving one's body and feet to the rhythm of beautiful music causes a feeling of ecstasy. All nations have their dancing and some of the Eastern dancing is graceful and some mad – although we are copying much of it.

I know we shall have recreation as well as work, so will you tell us something about it.

A fish swims, a bird flies, a human walks, runs and jumps. Why should you not dance?

I suppose we envisage becoming rather sedate on our higher level.

And you do not envisage laughing until tears flow. These sober thoughts of the heaven world have been ingrained into many of you from childhood. Why would you have been given the ability to laugh and dance, which, as you say, bring great joy, if you were not meant to do so?

Well, this earth plane is so different. We shall not kill and maim and cheat in heaven, so maybe we shall not find pleasure in some of the things that give us joy now. I have never heard of a Medium describing a departed soul as dancing or even singing.

There are a lot of things you have never heard of, including so much of what goes on in the next phase of your existence. When you were in kindergarten you had not heard of trigonometry and psychology! Unless you have travelled from your own country you cannot imagine the feel and the atmosphere of the East or the West. Hundreds of years ago there were no photographs, but you learned by word of mouth.

All is movement, all is rhythm. Your mortal body is beating, breathing, hearing, smelling, feeling, seeing. Your etheric body is scintillating, your soul body is positively 'dancing for joy'!

You think the *little* you is making this up because it doesn't seem 'down to earth' enough. Well, it isn't. We are not talking about your earth existence. You drop off your heavy body and become light as a feather and free as the air.

You, yourself, feel no sorrow for those who die, only thankfulness for their freedom. Your compassion is for those who remain encased in their temporary state.

Dear Ones, Wake Up. Life on earth is how you deal with it, how you live it. Life on the next plane is a 'walk-over' into glorious Light, wonderful Peace and the glow of Love all around you. And of course You Can Dance!

Iraq Revisited

I can only try to experience Iraq in my imagination and through television pictures. What a terrible disaster that Country has become. It is as if we had put out a fire and caused a flood we cannot deal with. God, what is the solution now?

You are trying to use your symbol of the golden rose to help you comprehend My answer. Your rose has its head down, its petals are limp and have lost their red tips and all around is grey and gloomy, giving you a feeling of sadness and helplessness.

This form of concern and sadness will not help anyone. Do you recall how you never lost your 'grit' during World War 11, even when you thought the Germans might overrun your Country?

My misguided people in all countries and all over your world continue to act with irresponsible motives. Do you try to heal a gaping wound by adding poisons and gravel and spikes, then declaring it is a cure – against your better judgment and that of the recipient? Would that recipient believe you were using love and understanding. And how much fright would you be creating? The fear is so strong in Iraq it ascends right up into the ether, not only from the Iraqis, but from those armed forces supposedly there to bring peace! The stench of Fear is blatant, ominous. And in spite of their grit, every man, woman and child in that Country is full of fear, including the armed forces, the terrorists and the charity workers.

How do you think those in other countries are feeling, who condone what they see and what they have caused? Excuses never dissolve actions.

Then there are those who really try to make amends, only to be met with resistance, as in Israel, Palestine, Northern Ireland, to name but a few.

All this happens because we have Free Will, yet how about the Free Will of those of us who do not condone fighting, even fox hunting? When told these things have gone on for centuries, why does that make it right? We used to have public beheading, the guillotine and gallows. Can a ride or a gallop not be enjoyed without a red coat, a stirrup cup and a tortured fox? This will not go down well with huntsmen and women, but where is their compassion? I could now be sick, literally, if I stood looking in a butcher's shop window, imagining myself biting into that bloody meat, yet I was not always a vegetarian. I like to think I have changed for the better.

You can each change yourselves, but you, alone, cannot change the world. This is where sincere, unselfish prayer can take over. You still do not realise that prayer is your strongest weapon, your most prized tool. Use it. I keep telling you this, just as I keep telling you so much is being achieved by prayer. Because you cannot see a great rainbow or a new bright star, do not – for a moment – lose heart, lose hope, or let in fear, because that diminishes some of your effort.

When you pray, know that it is a great force you are using. Know that right, honest prayer can do only good. You are not a voice 'crying out in the wilderness', you are one of millions, yes millions, helping to create Good and Peace and so bring about the ecstasy that I wish to experience through you. Become a responsible citizen, a responsible parent, a responsible writer, reader, speaker – BE, as I created you, in my image and likeness.

Forgiveness

God, I am finding it so difficult to understand the book, "The Disappearance of the Universe". Why? I can accept this life is a dream, but I do not understand about having so much to forgive myself for. It reminds me of the old statement that we are all born in sin. Do I delude myself when I feel contented and at peace? Much has happened in my life that could have made me sour, disillusioned, disappointed. But you know I do not hold any grudges and that I could have behaved very differently when under great strain. Please tell me about forgiveness.

Your golden rose, fully open and peaceful, has moved over to a seat and sat down in a thoughtful mood.

Readers will sometimes think I am bonkers when I see this sort of thing!

Does that matter? It is your way of listening and understanding.

You are looking back on your present life and trying to recall when you might have acted differently. You feel that you should have had more thought for your beloved mother when she broke her arm when you were in your teens. Did she suffer more because you carried on with your own life?

No, I don't think so because my father was there and we had sufficient domestic help.

Then you can let go of that one. Next?

I wish I hadn't let my sons go to boarding school, especially as I had hated it so much myself. One of them tolerated it and said afterwards that it had helped him to stand on his own feet, but the other loathed it.

And why did you send them? I will tell you; at that time you were working hard, admittedly in your home, but you and their father, after much thought, felt it would be beneficial for them to have that discipline if they were to do well educationally. They were so engrossed in their electronics when at home they did not give sufficient thought to other subjects. Do you think they reproach you for sending them away?

I don't know. One wrote to his father in later life and mentioned that home for him became like a holiday resort more than what home is to most people. I find that sad.

Ask him about it.

I will. I wonder if that will make me feel better or worse.

I recall something I did that was unkind and thoughtless. I have remembered this many times. After my retirement, when my elderly husband was needing much help, one morning when I was bathing him, I rubbed his back rather hard in a bit of frustration. He glanced up at me. We said nothing. That was unforgivable of me because he was the most patient, loving soul imaginable. I probably hurt him deeply. He would never have done that to me. I think he now knows my feelings about this and that I ask his forgiveness.

When I started this conversation with you, dear God, I wasn't expecting it to be a bit like this. What are you trying to make me understand?

90

My child, you are deeply upset at this moment. Do you think there may be those who are deeply upset by their treatment of you? You recall one who came to you through a medium some years ago, asking for forgiveness. You were shocked, surprised, for you held no malice. You declared, "Yes, of course I forgive you."

This has become a very personal experience. It has upset my equilibrium.

Ah, you see. You have learned how important forgiveness is.

Yes, but I knew that kind of forgiveness is important. It seems there is another kind that I do not understand.

Are there two kinds of Love? Are there two kinds of Forgiveness?

'Forgive us our trespasses as we forgive those who trespass against us'

'Forgive us our debts as we forgive our debtors'.

Peace, my child. Do you know you hurt Me when you hurt yourselves! I feel that anguish and I say, "Peace, peace. All is well, now and forever".

Thank you my beloved Friend.

Know Your Power

It appears as if the gold rose is indicating – just open the book and see what turns up. So I await today's message with a 'clean slate', wondering what I will be told.

There is absolute silence yet you are not at peace. You are letting world events get to you. You are feeling inadequate, frustrated, despondent.

When you feel this way, all of you, go deeper within. This life is temporary, but you can either pass through it unnoticed or leave your mark. Your circumstances limit you to a certain extent, but you can rise above them and take that overview.

How much worthwhile thought do you use in a day? Are you dwelling on the petty, the unimportant? Some people and events are out of your hands and you think you can only look on.

Here is your opportunity to use your intelligence, your higher knowing, your connection with Spirit.

The difference you can make is by knowing the Truth, living the Truth and speaking the Truth. Never mind that some people put you down, make you question your beliefs. That is good. Every now and again you need to think deeply, to check up on your thoughts. You connect with your Truth deep within you and there you find your answers, your comfort, your strength.

Remain open to guidance, but not to criticism. Let the trivial float over you, not through you. Remember your roots are deep enough to withstand the gales, the buffeting, even great storms. That is when you are tested and you know you can keep calm, awaiting the calm after the storms.

When you have reached the stage where you can read these words and find your own peace and comfort, you have reached another stage of advancement. You are ready for more testing, more experience, more Truth.

Your right thought and actions get added to the weight of Good and the scales are toppling over with that weight, and as it pours out you can add more and more of the good, first class ingredients to keep the good overflowing and pouring down upon the earth.

There it is added to, again and again, and goes back onto the scales. Good attracts Good. Whatever job you are doing you can use good thoughts. If it is a manual or menial job you can do some deep thinking while you are about your other work. If your work requires great attention, great concentration, you can tune-in to the power of Good before you commence each task. You can place yourself in that channel of Light which lets true knowledge pour in, thus enabling you to do what is best, right, effective. There are two ways to do any job – well or indifferently.

Since all that you do is a picking up of knowledge from its source, is it not easier to tap into that Source first, then let the knowledge flow through you? Man can spend hours, days or even years trying to fathom what sometimes seems the impossible. Then one day everything falls into place and he thinks, 'why didn't I think of that earlier?' Man does not invent, he discovers. Shall we go back to the previous thoughts that we haven't mentioned lately? Namely, see the finished article, see it as perfect, then give it thought in the creating of it, then draw the plans or gather the tools or think about the beginnings.

That is what *you* have done today. You *knew* there was a message; you imagined it created. Then you cleared your mortal mind of clutter, knowing you would 'hear' My words; then you placed your hands on your computer, already switched on, and knew your thoughts would drive your fingers to create the data, ready for the finished article to be read.

Only a short time ago you thought there was nothing there, but deep down you knew the Truth.

So with your help for your world. See perfect peace reigning, know that you can be used to help make it manifest, then collect your thoughts and put them into a Prayer for Peace. And the more often you use your prayers for Peace the sooner it will come.

Never feel helpless; do not accept less than the best. Know your Power.

To Each His Own Dream

My golden rose is appearing perfect. It is fully open, upright and still. What is that telling me, dear God?

It is showing you that in spite of recent happenings your life is calm and serene. You have put into practice what you know is true, namely that All Is Well Now. You remembered to turn every negative thought into a positive one. You replaced one with the other, just as you are going to replace your car with another. You know you are typing this before you have had confirmation and so this is a test of your acceptance of My words.

You will be stronger through this experience and better able to help yourself and others in the future – that future which is really Now.

You are remembering that nothing happens by Chance; there are no Accidents. You have recalled elsewhere how the pieces of the jig-saw which has formed your present life are pieces you would never have dreamed of putting together. Now you can look back and see how the pieces fit together.

You tried recently to add some pieces that you felt sure were going into place, but you jumped too far ahead – you didn't see the nearer picture. Nothing was lost – except one book, and who knows where that is!

I am sure You know where that book is and I just hope it has 'happened' to reach a receptive reader who will benefit from it.

As White Eagle says, Keep on Keeping on. All the suffering you are witnessing is affecting only the mortal mind and body. All my beloved children Will wake up from their dream. Let each soul dream its own dream, but be there when you are needed to help them Wake Up.

Rising Above the Earthly Mind

God, my life doesn't get easier. I am tired of rowing against the tide. Where am I going wrong?

Go right into your rose of Peace and feel its petals around you, soft, yet strong in their protection. You, all of you, become vulnerable when you do not wrap up against the cold or protect yourselves from heat.

Earthly conditions, earthly thoughts, are so much what you make them with your mortal mind. Rise above the turmoil, the unrest, the little worries – for they are small worries, little fears which you allow to take hold of your Being. In a year, in a month, in a week, all can change and most times you forget what you were concerned about.

As to the bigger issues, you deal with those in the manner to which you have become accustomed, namely, you drag them along like a wet towel or you try to pass them on to someone else or you remember to hand them over to Me.

When you watch a child hurt itself you know it will get better or you take it to a doctor; inwardly your best treatment is to see that child perfect again, even if the injury is so severe that it does not survive its present life.

That, you think, sounds hard and cruel. Now look on, from My view point. All is well NOW and you will wake up from your dream to find perfection – to see your life as the dream that it was. You are in a temporary phase. The death and destruction you witness across your world are an illusion.

Give of yourself to yourself and to others in the way of compassion, understanding, comfort and, above all, Love. Do not expect everyone to feel as you do for their feelings depend on their attitude to, and understanding of, Life as they see it . Those of you who can rise above the earthly mind are indeed blessed.

Not only is there No Death, there is No Thing to fear. Fear is only fear of the unknown and deep within there is no unknown. All knowledge is within you. It is up to you, it is your Free Will, to look for that knowledge. How would you know there were bluebells in the wood if you did not seek them for yourself? Others can tell you they are there, but experiencing their truth, their being, is reality.

Oh, my children, there is untold joy awaiting you all and your present seeming existence will become as nothing. Use the imagination I gave you to prepare for your real life – in a perfect body of Light in a perfect state of perpetual ecstasy.

Hierarchy

A questioner wishes to know about hierarchy on the higher planes. Would you please explain this?

You will find there are no 'bosses' as such on higher planes, think of it more as putting colours in a certain order. They are different, but are all colours. You aspire to certain 'ranks', but that does not mean one soul is more important than another – more knowledgeable, yes, in their particular choice of understanding.

Where all is Love there can be no seniority, but there is great respect one for another according to their understanding of a subject or method or complexity. You would not expect to find everyone studying the same subject or making seeming progress in the same direction. All choose to expand their knowledge, which is still an inner knowing.

There is great joy in achievement, just as on the earth plane, and souls move on according to their desire and readiness. There are teachers and guides and helpers, but they consider themselves equal and all knowledge is accepted as a privilege. There are no examinations, no competition, only a gentle progression according to each soul's choice. There is also a remembering of what you would now call the past.

There are similes on your earth plane. At school you have a curriculum and must study many subjects and take examinations. Then at University you choose your preferred subjects to specialise in and more advanced teachers help you to gain your goals. Often on your way you discover something you were not expecting and it becomes a great delight to you.

There are subjects to interest every soul, from the seeming least evolved to the most highly evolved, then the latter move on, sometimes returning to help those on lower planes, including the earth plane.

There is never a dull moment! This does not mean you spend all your time studying. There are countless paths to follow and many are sheer joy and entertainment and even serious studying is no ordeal for your capacity to imbibe knowledge is much greater than you experience now in this world.

You do not need to give 'titles' to more highly evolved Beings, you intuitively recognise their greater knowledge and automatically revere them.

All is done with Love, unselfish, pure Love with no thought for self, only a giving. Only a desire to Give and that giving returns as Love.

Attaining the Impossible

I have been given several on-going questions to ask since receiving Your message about hierarchy. I am trying to push away what I personally feel about these because some of my own answers must be just conjecture. Please help me to be sure I am making my own mortal mind quiet, so that I receive Your answers through a pure channel of Truth.

You are seeing your yellow rose against a background of blue space – nothing else in view. You find this conflicts with your knowledge of no time nor space, but in this case the picture is conveying the vastness of the Whole. You are aeons away from the Oneness you are trying to grasp.

We go back to the picture of the little ant on the garden path where it experiences such a long journey from path to pond, let alone wondering about where the sunshine comes from. That is beyond its present power of understanding.

So with your human understanding. There is only so much you can absorb at this earth level. A few of you delve into the possible workings of outer space and some of your theories are correct, but much is surmise and false conjecture.

When you rise from the earth plane you leave behind your heavy bodies and re-clothe yourselves in a much lighter body of different elements. You return to a familiar scene, where you have 'lived' many times before. Sometimes, when you reincarnate to earth, you have the gift of remembering past earth lives and a good memory of the higher plane you have left.

There comes a time when you no longer need, nor wish, to return to this earthy, unevolved plane, but to enjoy the heaven world, the summerland, and desire to learn more about the next higher plane. You do this easily because you now know there is no death as such, but a moving-on.

Just as many of you meditate on this earth plane and 'see' pictures of planes you know are 'higher', so you do this on each successive plane, only now you are sometimes taken to a higher plane for a glimpse of what is to come. This is done by a higher soul who has descended in order to help you progress. All is progress, all is movement; you only 'stand still' if you wish to do so, just as now you know people who are quite satisfied to live each day without thinking about any future. There is nothing wrong with that, especially if you are satisfied and grateful for what you have, but there comes a time in every life, in every incarnation, when the soul wishes to know more. It is natural for adults to have an enquiring nature, just as a child does.

How many planes are there? Why do I connect the number seven with this?

Of course there are seven, you have seven mountains and seven rivers on the earth plane, but that does not mean the total. I have to remind you of your present limitation of acceptable knowledge because you are not capable of absorbing more than a certain amount of the Allness. Go back to the little ant. Think of the little child, just starting at school. Now go into your innermost and realise that even there you find a limit as to how much you can 'imagine'. You cannot imagine eternity, you even feel you will get tired if life goes on and on. Doesn't this prove you have limitations?

When do souls stop separating themselves from oneness?

You can begin to experience that on the earth plane. With some people you feel a great warmth, a one-ness, *en rapport*, a blending. Then maybe you attend a large meeting of like souls where you are all imbibing a 'same' uplifting message or theory and you feel at-one with everybody else. You experience a love for one another, even though earlier on you were strangers, so you thought. Thought, you see, is enabling you to blend, to experience a new experience! You are getting an inkling of being All One.

When we become All One in aeons of Time (which doesn't exist anyway) what will we experience, for we shall have no goal? Where will be pleasure or satisfaction or Life?

I can only describe to your presently immature minds the occasional experiences you have in your present lifetimes when you are so happy that you wish 'time would stand still'. Those precious moments that 'are too good to be true'. When you experience utter contentment, true peace, bliss. That is when you will be One With Me.

A Cosmic Career

Another question I have been asked is whether we have some sort of Cosmic Career Plan and, if so, what influences it. Please use me.

Your golden rose is scrabbling about in a lot of dead leaves and undergrowth and its antics are making you smile. What do *you* think it is telling you?

It is obviously looking for something. This comic side of our conversations always amazes me as I still feel I should be serious. I still fear being inadequate for deep answers.

When will you realise, and accept, that all My answers are deep? It is the eventual reader that either takes in their depth or just reads them 'on the surface'.

Your rose is telling you that, while on the earth plane, you are ever searching. First you search for your real role in this life – sometimes failing to find it or follow it. Then as you progress you wonder about your next, higher phase of existence. Some of you begin to anticipate what you would like to do.

Even having spent years of study, a doctor will sometimes change his or her career for something different; a logger will become a poet. Circumstances or memories may cause these changes.

As you rise through the cosmic planes the vastness makes you realise why you needed to return to each plane so many times in order to imbibe sufficiency. Again I have to remind you how comparatively simple the earth plane is and how difficult it is for you, at your present stage, to visualise much higher spheres.

The ultimate Cosmic Plan is to return to the Whole, which is Me. So the Career Plan embraces everything you can conceive of. You will experience All, but you cannot conceive of that yet.

Take each step as it comes. Take each day as it comes. As you do so be conscious of loving guidance 'each step of the way'. Pray for fulfilment of your highest level of Knowing at each phase you are at in the Now.

Incarnations

Before incarnating, do we really choose, more or less, what our path will be like? If so, does that mean the more difficulties we encounter the more progress we make towards a higher plane?

Behind your golden rose is a long line of similar roses becoming smaller and smaller, indicating a regressing into the past or a progressing into the present.

You return with a rough sketch of the picture you wish to paint. The important features are already drawn in – for example large buildings, near and distant views, a certain number of people. This is in black and white with little detail.

As you live your present life you fill in the colours and the details. You not only look AT the buildings, you move INTO them; you not only see the views, you travel across them.

En route you experience the detail; each tiny blade of grass, each path, all weather conditions. You encounter many of the people because you *chose* to re-associate with them. Some of the scenery you have experienced before; some of the paths you have trodden before; some of the paths you have avoided before.

Just as now, you may decide to paint your house white or redesign your garden or to plant fruit trees instead of vegetables, so you experience different aspects, new venues.

How you react depends therefore on what you have chosen. Mostly you feel you have made an improvement; sometimes you do not approve of the result.

This is a very simple explanation of a very important event. You are being given the chance to re-live, to re-think your life. Just as in a picture every brush stroke makes a difference to the whole, so in your life every act, every word, every thought affects your overall Being.

You have returned with much inner knowing. The work of an artist usually improves with practice, but sometimes he ceases painting or she alters her style into something quite bizarre. Occasionally you 'lose the plot' as you say or go off at a tangent, but the original sketch is there in black and white. It is a blueprint of what you hoped to achieve in this lifetime.

From the original sketch a masterpiece can be achieved – progress you thought impossible, giving joy to thousands. But they are exceptions and not the rule.

So we should be very careful how we use our free will, our free choice?

You begin to see, to realise, how your every move alters the scene, sometimes for the better, sometimes for the worse.

Your sketch may be very sparse – almost a 'blank canvas' – or it may already show great detail, with only a few more brush strokes required. It may show many places of worship – churches, mosques, synagogues, that you decide to visit this time round – and perhaps you find your real Being out in the open, under the stars, free from ritual and ceremonial.. Then maybe you feel a great urge to return 'home' where all is peace and love, without rules and regulations, without war and conflict, without vice and stealth.

The ultimate longing, deep within all my children, is to live in perfection and Love.

Worry & Concern

I know worrying is a waste of energy, but surely concern is a kind of worrying? If we are 'feeling' individuals we cannot help being concerned for those near to us when they are unwell or stressed, unhappy or taking what we can see is the wrong path.

Your life is one big experience made up of a lot of little experiences. Your free choice gives you the opportunity to experience and experiment and in so doing you weave the intricate pattern that becomes your life chart. A map has countless roads and lanes, rivers and brooks, towns and villages, mountains and valleys. By travelling about you make your life interesting, but you also find thickets and dead ends which cause you to take a different route.

Sometimes you are advised not to go along a certain path, but a little inner tweak suggests you try it for yourself. Often you learn the hard way, but it impresses you more than if you had just done what someone else suggested.

You guide little children, you guide the blind, you warn others of dangers, but you still cannot live their lives for them. Therefore you need to look on, without being concerned, and hope your loved one or friend will cope with the consequences.

That hope can be a prayer. It *does* make a difference when you pray for another, unselfishly, for you place them in the Light and if they are receptive their inner knowing responds to that Light, that Guidance. At best it guides them to a better route, at least it gives them strength to endure their situation.

If you were that person you would act differently, but you are not. They are their own person and consequently they go their own path, either accepting the consequences or fighting against them. They are learning more from their free choice than if they just followed what another tells them to do. The goal post doesn't move. You reach it along the plains or you get caught up in the brambles, the rough sea, sometimes severe storms, but you usually come through stronger for the experience.

Therefore, do not be concerned for others in the way that you were meaning. Be caring, be understanding, be there for them, but do not fear for them. Worry is fear and you know how fear is your enemy. You have nothing, no thing, to fear, for you are never alone or out of My Mind.

Bless you my beloved children.

The True Son

God, the first of two questions I have been asked. Why did your Son, Jesus, wish to leave You?

My children, you are All my sons and daughters and, just as you do not wish to stay on the earth plane forever, so will you not wish to stay for ever on the next plane, and the next, and the next.

Your instinct is inquisitive; it never rests. Your very Being wishes to go on or go back in order to put something right or to experience more or to help others on their path.

Those who have returned to your planet as a mighty Teacher can be likened to those who enter the Olympic Games in order to achieve their highest goal. They wish to become masters of their trade. So with those you call great Masters through the ages, they have wished to return to show you the way, to be an example, not for their own good, but for your advancement. They have a great desire to enable you to move on.

My beloved son, Jesus, was one such and others have been back whom you have looked upon as great Beings, namely Buddha, Mohammed, Krishna, Ghandi, and many others who have been forgotten. It is within all of you to become great masters. You are all of the same essence. As soon as you start to seek the Truth you put your foot on the first rung of the ladder and as you see Good, act Good, Be good, so you advance up that ladder.

Sometimes you climb an unhelpful ladder and after some ascent you halt. You do not find all the answers and you start to make up some of the text so that it fits in with your preconceived ideas. This is how so many religions have developed. They all commence from the Truth, but they stray from it, adding this and that, but without continuing to use the Essence.

Most of the descended Masters have previously gone far beyond the next plane. Then they have a great longing to return, with immense selflessness, to help their lesser-informed brothers and sisters. Jesus preached to All of you. His example and lessons were for All of you. And the great Love he brought forth from the people of that time has grown and grown and continued to grow and continued to make sense to those who have come since. That is why His Teachings, His example, have lived on, making, causing, you to follow.

There are those of you on earth now who will return to higher planes than others, either because you descended from there or because you have progressed further than some others while on earth.

As I have told you many times, all is movement, all is progress, all is experience.

This is beautiful and fits in with some lives, but how can we still, after all these thousands of years, have millions of starving and homeless people, increasing by the day? Of course I am referring particularly to the terrible plight of those in the Sudan, fleeing from Darfur. Their suffering is beyond description and is only realised by us through our television screens. And why is so little being done to help them?

My children, you do not practise true unselfishness. You still take more than you give. There are those who stand up for animal rights – and they do get heard – but how many stand up for humanity's rights and get heard.? How many are truly willing to go without, even just a little, to make the lives of those with nothing, more humane? All they ask is for food and shelter, be it of the most primitive kind. What would my Son, Jesus, have said and done about that?

I think He would have said, "Leave all, follow Me, love your neighbour as yourself".

The Ego

The second question. Where does the Ego come from?

The ego is the little you that likes to feel important. It separates itself from the higher you in order to be that – separate. Then it gets itself, in other

102

words you, into difficulties. It cannot 'stand on its own two feet', it gets knocked down like a 'house of cards' and it doesn't like that.

I understand that, but where does it come from?

It comes from being dissatisfied with Who You Really Are. You have brown hair and you bleach it. You have instinct which tells you right from wrong, but you don't always like being told that, so you go against 'nature'. You can use the ego to draw attention to yourself – an example of wanting to be apart.

By using your ego you are shutting out your Higher Mind. You are choosing to be egotistical!

But did You put it there?

Did I give you corns? Did I give you indigestion? Did I make you stressed?

I gave you a perfect body, right food, enough time, but you abuse these gifts by thinking you know better, by taking what you think is a chance, by jumping without forethought. The ego is the outcome of wrong thinking, wrong acting, misconceptions.

Some people's egos 'stick out a mile', some are so small they are hardly noticeable.

Do animals have egos?

To a lesser extent. A fledging can try to fly too early; a dog can try to be clever beyond its capabilities; a kitten can fall off a wall. These are small mammals. You will notice large animals displaying less egotism.

Then why are we, as fairly large and intelligent animals, so prone to use our egos?

You have a more intricate intelligence and you do so like to be *right*. It is your persistent desire to be right that encourages your ego to jump in.

To wonder if *I* gave you your ego is like asking if I gave you your indigestion or your corn or your stress. There is Cause and Effect and that applies to practically everything you do and think and it applies to the use of the ego.

Think about this, deeply.

Armageddon

God, I do not feel at all adequate to ask you about Armageddon. To me it is a man-made myth. Please help.

This is when you think about looking up references in other writings, checking what your Bible says and generally going round in circles.

You are afraid to trust yourself to put down what I tell you.

Of course your world as you know it will change; of course there will be climatic changes and man-made changes and what you call catastrophes. Man does not heed warning signs when it means making his life less comfortable.

When wars cause the death of thousands of people, what do you think happens to them? Do some of you still think those souls hang about awaiting a Judgment Day? Do you think they are nowhere for a time? Some of you believe all 'dead' souls are awaiting a grand awakening.

You are NEVER DEAD. You just leave your cloak behind. So whatever awaits you in your future you will survive, either on earth or on your next plane. Your old enemy, FEAR, tries to fill your little mind with thoughts of ghastly happenings.

You see the result of earthquakes, volcanic eruptions, floods, terrorism, explosions. Those left on the earth plane cope with these situations, horrific as they seem, sometimes causing a great bond between the suffering, mourning and injured. You are Survivors. Do not meet trouble halfway – better by far to deal with present traumas and pray for strength to deal with each situation in your life as and when it arises.

You are never alone, you are never apart from ME, you are never forgotten. More positively I would say you are always in MY care, MY Mind, and you do best to take each day as it comes, using your Knowing of how best to deal with every situation. Cast out Fear, and Trust instead.

A Pause for Thought

So how are we doing? If you have read as far as this you must be absorbing something you consider is worthwhile.

I wonder what your thoughts and beliefs were before you started? I think you were a seeker and when we are seekers the right books and meetings and even people 'get in our way'. One reader told me my last book literally fell off the shelf into her hands!

An occurrence that amazes me – there are a few books I pick up at random and open at random and *always* the helpful message is there; the answer to some problem; an explanation for a query; a statement of simple fact. Thus the Higher Mind takes over from the lower and deals with a situation, often telling me to let go, let God.

Recently I had to deal with a legal business problem and, though I had referred to a particular book for more than thirty years, I do not remember ever reading before words that said, 'You do not need to attempt to stand up for your 'rights'. Realise that God adjusts things with exact law, and peace will return to your heart." In other words, if only we will remember to hand everything over to God we have no problems.

It just seems too simple to be true, but it works. We waste so much thought and energy unnecessarily when we could put them to better use.

We also waste much of our time reading and watching utter rubbish. I am not talking about funny books and programmes that do us good, because we need to laugh and be light-hearted. I am talking about idiotic items that are particularly lacking in real humour and common decency.

Are we beginning to understand how powerful we are? How our thoughts and prayers can alter and help our world? How important it is that we choose right leaders in all high places; those who will put self last and others – in all countries – first. Are we querying old and new laws to make sure they are good for everyone? Or are we just sitting back and letting others rule us, feeling ineffectual to do anything ourselves.

Sometimes making ourselves heard is a great effort. Recently I wrote a dozen letters about Living Wills, also called Advance Directives. This entailed visiting the library for help with titles and addresses, but if only a few of those letters get noticed it may help us to take control of our end days. I am not talking about euthanasia, but about being kept alive against our wishes.

When you contact your Inner Knowing about our eternal lives, why should we stay here any longer than is necessary and natural? We are only a breath away from our original home. And there is absolutely no doubt that we shall return there.

And there is no wrathful God awaiting us. Only Good, and that Good will cause us to judge ourselves and treat ourselves accordingly.

Free Will

God, why am I again experiencing reluctance in tuning-in to You? I know the questions I wish to ask and I am sure You will give me answers, so why this reluctance?

My child, you are reluctant because you already know what my answers will be. They are answers that you are now able to give from your gained knowledge and they do not satisfy the scientists, the anthropologists, the archaeologists – in other words the 'know alls'. Ask away.

Was Atlantis a place or a myth?

You lived there!

Wait a minute. You haven't even answered my question.

Not only did you live there; you were a very powerful entity in a position of great authority. You witnessed technology and communication far beyond what you all experience today. There were thousands of individuals who also thought they 'knew it all' at that time. They too lived for the present without considering the future. They too were given signs, intimations, that their technology was getting above their understanding. They too took risks without using their inner knowing, their intuition, that maybe they should slow down and listen to wisdom from within.

And yes, they did destroy themselves and their land. They upset the delicate balance of nature. Mortal man ever wants to be quicker, richer, more clever, without spending enough thought on the consequences.

White Eagle has told about that ancient world in some of his teachings and Tom Hartmann tells of the present situation in 'The Last Hours of Ancient Sunlight'.

Maybe that is why I have these strong feelings about this subject – partly because I was there and partly because of these writings I have read in this life. So now I ask, why has there been this terrific earthquake under the sea and the ghastly tsunami that has killed, maimed and made homeless thousands and thousands of human beings? Is man partly to blame in this case or is it, as we are being told, something that happens every 50,000 years or so?

If you drop a soft ball of wool from your hand on to the carpet, think for a moment what has taken place. Your hand is a fraction lighter, the air moved as the ball fell, a small space above the carpet has become filled by a ball of wool. Even the surface of the carpet has become slightly altered. And *all that* has happened just from dropping a few metres of wool. A plane flies over your garden on a calm day and the air it moved causes a temporary breeze across the land you are standing on, even though that plane is many feet above. Is it therefore not feasible to consider what effect is happening in the sea and on the earth and in the atmosphere by man's bombing and testing and extracting?

But why do you let us move faster than our understanding, thereby allowing us to kill all these innocent people, especially the children?

Why do you make such poor use of your Free Will? I gave you that as a precious gift, to make you feel good, to cause you joy, to let you experience Freedom. Instead you let it imprison you in an unhealthy body in a foul atmosphere, living in dread of the future and afraid of dying! You put faith in tobacco and drugs, hoping or believing they will make you happier; you choose to eat items that alter your shape; you choose to drink alcohol until you are not fully conscious; you force yourselves to stay awake when your body indicates it needs sleep; you exercise beyond bodily endurance. Oh my children, have you heard of discipline?

Now I know this does not apply to all of you, but would you agree that it is beginning to apply to the majority? If I took away your Free Will now you would be like zombies. Would you learn or progress?

It is natural for a baby to want to crawl, then to stand, then to walk, then to run, then to speak and to listen and to learn. What has happened to man's desire to better himself instead of standing still? And those who race ahead in science and electronics have a desire to achieve more and more, but they are not stopping to think of consequences. Just as a child must not run across a busy street, so a 'clever' man or woman must stop to look where they are heading, what results ensue, how others are involved or might be affected.

Along with your Free Will you need to keep your intelligence ahead of you. The more good you achieve the better your landing on the next plane, otherwise you will find yourself in a thick fog of confusion. It is up to each one of you where you land.

Removing the Clutter

God, why do we put off doing jobs that we know have to be done?

Your rose has slipped off the wall and hidden out of sight on the other side. What is this telling you?

That I don't want to look at it right now.

Exactly. You knew you had to sort out some practical jobs and you wanted to put them off. Now you have got those jobs out of the way, you feel better and able to get on with more important work.

The mortal mind, the mortal body, tend to be lazy. It is natural to want to do pleasurable things and put off the mundane, that is partly why some people are untidy and careless. It takes effort and discipline to be 'organised', yet this is important to progress. You cannot progress well along a path strewn with litter and brambles. Clear the way and you can run through, clear-headed, wondering why you put off the manual and menial work that needed to be done.

You progress better when your mind is clear and when there is no clutter to interfere with your clear thinking. Your line of communication has to be clear if you are to hear the true notes, the true message, the unhindered thought waves.

Just as a child needs discipline and order in its life in order to learn and progress, so adults require to throw out the unnecessary objects that just get in their way.

Trees and shrubs shed their old leaves, clearing the way for new growth. Flowers drop their dead petals so as not to waste energy holding on to them when that energy is needed for new development. Animals lose hair from their coats to enable new hair to come through, just as your yourselves shed your hair and your worn nails and your dead layers of skin.

Remember about all being movement. Shed the old outworn ideas and make room for the new. When a room becomes full of junk, there is no room for new furniture and you are unable to find articles you need amidst the clutter. Weeds choke and cover up what really matters in a garden; they prevent new growth.

You didn't want to weed your computer files, yet it took you twice as long to find what was important. Now you feel uplifted by your effort.

Now you are ready to move forward with a clear mind, ready to hear what comes through your higher mind.

Not only your land, but your Mind also needs to become fertile in order to put forth the seeds that I drop into it – and that applies to all who read these words. You would not be reading them if you were not anxious and willing to absorb more worthwhile knowledge. Deep within you have a strong desire to progress. Make sure the way is clear.

The Unthinking Man's Idol

I have been asked 'how vital is it that we stop listening to the ego?'

Listening to the ego is kidding yourself. The ego tells you what you want to think at that moment. The little you, which is the ego, wants to be right about everything, from telling yourself you are beautiful to believing you are ugly and unwanted; it tells you you are right in what you are doing and thinking at that particular moment; it tells you what you want to hear – yes even when you think you don't want to hear it! It is the unthinking man's idol. Her yardstick, his righteousness.

The ego can appear to improve with age, to become more self-righteous, to become the boss.

Quell the ego and what do you find? A nothingness? A loss?

No, you hear that quieter, more thoughtful you. It was there all the time, but you didn't give it a chance to make itself heard. And as you listen you hear more, you think more deeply, you understand another's point of view, you experience unselfishness, you listen more and say less.

In this newer state you realise you are not always right. You realise there are so often other ways to go. You find your Higher Mind is much superior to your ego, which is your little mind.

It is now that you turn negative thoughts into positive ones. The Higher Mind attracts like to itself. Life changes from trivial to meaningful. You discover you have a power that the little ego doesn't like. The little ego learns to take a back seat. It finds it wasn't as clever and right as it thought it was. This newly found Mind doesn't have to 'make up' solutions, invent situations, be right.

The Higher Mind knows all already. The Higher Mind knows it is part of Good. You recall the words of one of your hymns, "God be in my head and in my understanding". And I am in your heart and in your thinking. Use me.

Tuning In

Our lives would be so much simpler if only we would remember that You are always with us, knowing our every thought and every move. We let our minds ramble about wondering what to do and where to go, causing us frustration, doubt, confusion and disappointment.

Then a nudge comes, we let in the Light, a book opens at just the right page to get us on course, and we hand over all that was worrying us.

Why do we make it so unnecessarily hard for ourselves?

As I say so often, you forget to remember. You return to earth with deep knowledge. It is the kind of knowledge that you do not require while you are in babyhood, but some of it makes itself known to you when you are still very young. You accept, unquestioning, some of this instinct yet adults humour you and think you are making up a lot of nonsense. You see nature spirits and glimpses of the life you have just left and you accept this. It is when you try to talk about it that others 'put you down' so you shut off.

Later in life you re-connect with your higher self and to some it comes quite easily and they progress fast; others have to seek hard and long to convince themselves that they are on the right track.

Once you get on that track life takes on a completely different meaning and appearance. But you still lapse from this higher state and grovel about 'on your own'.

It is when you remember that I am always with you – you are never alone – then you become conscious that your guide or guides and teachers are with you. These beings are so loving that they wish only for your good and often they are referred to as angels. It gives them great pleasure to be 'used'. They wish only for your good and advancement. That innate instinct, that is so important in you, needs to be used because there are some earthly souls who will try to lead you astray, point you in the wrong direction. But you know Truth when you hear it.

Could we come to rely too much on handing everything over so that our problems do not have to be solved by us?

You will find that does not happen. You can be given a piano, sheets of all kinds of music and a teacher, but unless you put into practice what that teacher is telling you no melody is forthcoming. However, if you have a great desire to succeed you will not sit back, you will spend time and energy in trying to do well, sometimes changing your teacher, then maybe altering or adding to your instrument. You have learned much along the way, but not without help.

Ask for help in all the important things that you endeavour to do. That way you will advance quicker, with less likelihood of mistakes that have to be rectified. Keep that open, trusting Mind. Seek and you will find, ask and it shall be given to you. You have already knocked and entered when you initially sought out the Truth in the first instance.

Lack of Understanding

I have been asked 'Do we unconsciously fear God?'

You consciously fear God, Me, because that is the way most of you, of most religions, have been brought up. Your unconscious mind knows better! That is the simple answer.

Why would you fear Good – who wants nothing more for you but your Good? Do you fear Love? No, because you know Love is kind, beautiful, desirable, giving, understanding, gentle. Now remember Love is God, God is Love, God is Good.

Why do we experience lack?

Because you think you want what you have not got. A want is not always a need.

But how about the thousands who are without food, homes, land, work?

Who caused that? Some of *you* did because you wanted and took what was not yours, causing others to suffer and go without. There is more than enough for all my children and some are satisfied – and happy – with very little.

How about those who are without because of the tsunami and other catastrophes?

Those events bring out the best that is within my children. Suffering brings out endurance, bravery, unselfishness, loving and giving, compassion with a capital C, generosity. Despair can be changed into Hope. Thoughtfulness grows. The Power of Prayer is used. Even the hardened hearts are softened. Good overcomes seeming Evil. Few are unaffected in some way by these events. All is not lost. It is difficult for you to understand that Good really can evolve from such seeming disaster.

What is the impact of condemnation?

Who condemns? It is not Me. Condemnation is lack of understanding. There is a reason why some condemn others and a reason why some let themselves be condemned.

This subject requires much thought. Why do you condemn? Condemnation is used against those who appear not to comply with your standard of behaviour. Why does the condemned behave like that? Probably through lack of understanding or knowledge or example. Had that condemned man or woman been brought up in love they would not have behaved so. Therefore who are you to condemn them? You were privileged, they were not.

Take away all weapons, tie hands and feet, forbid shouting, then see what quiet conversation can bring forth. You do not expect there to be weapons in heaven, but do you think you will immediately agree with everyone else? No, you will have discussions, you will explain, listen, be willing to give in.

You can think about this for yourselves. You can think about why condemned people behaved as they did. You can use calm intelligence and in time that brings forth compassion. You can feel sorry for the suffering that the condemned is going through. Think how punishment has changed through the years – more thought has been used.

You, yourself, were amazed to see how *ornate* weapons used to be. The work that went into their make-up, be it swords, daggers, pistols. Weapons were possessions of pride and high office, yet all were made to kill. Battles and wars are portrayed as glorious victories, the pride of nations!

How far have you progressed on a path of Peace and Love, my children?

Devastation

God, you tell me what to write about today instead of me asking you questions.

You feel heavy-hearted child. You are thinking of the tsunami, Iraq, Darfur and the re-showing of the atrocities at Auschwitz sixty years ago.

Be thankful that you are not, and were not, in any of these places. Be thankful that you know how to help, for you do help with your donations and your prayers. There are millions of my people praying for Peace and you surely know now that prayer does help. You cannot see the prayers, the love and the compassion, but they are there in all those areas and in all those unselfish helpers who are there in body as well as spirit.

Your prayers rise up then flood the earth with hope and comfort amidst the devastation. And all the millions who have 'died' are above the turmoil, in peace and at peace on a higher plane. They wish you could feel their relief and happiness. They have left their dream, their nightmare. They have returned 'home'.

But what of those millions who are still on this plane, suffering, mourning, permanently injured? And they are homeless and jobless.

And they are learning. Yes, the hard way, but they are progressing. They are experiencing care and love from others; they are giving others the opportunity of using their selflessness. Try to accept that there is beauty amidst the horror.

Be strong, do not let the gloom get to you, only in so far that it makes *you* better beings. See Light, see Peace, not only over these places of horror and destruction, but over those in charge of the clearing up operation. And especially over the leaders of ALL countries in your world. Greed still rears its ugly head, where compassion and peace should be ruling.

Never has your world needed to take more heed of Guidance. The warning signs are being ignored by the many – who think only of today and the next few years. Pray that Minds will open up to the guidance that is being poured down, ready to show you better ways of living, eating, travelling, sharing and, above all, living together as a Whole. You are individuals, yet you are all One. And you will find you are all One at the next stage of your journey.

But there is no need to wait for the next stage, in fact there is not time (in your sense of time) to wait for the next stage – your return home.

All this knowledge is within you now. Some of you have lived through experiences like these in past lives.

Wake up from your dreams and nightmares. Live in the glory of Who You Really Are. Stop wanting what is not yours. Give instead of take. Every one of you possesses the mightiest weapon of all; it will never let you down; it will see you through every phase and seeming difficulty; it will never tarnish or become blunt. It is called LOVE. It overcomes all fear; it never harms. You cannot leave it behind, but you do forget to use it. You need it for every job you do and the more difficult the job the more you need it. It works in all situations. Use it – continuously.

Finding Our Way

It does seem incredible that there are so many religions and each one thinks it is right and the only one that should be followed.

Each one has some truth in it, each one has contradictions in it as well as contradictions with all the others.

God, how much longer is it going to take for us All to realise how wrong we are in so much of what we believe?

When an artist paints a picture, then realises not only is the perspective wrong but the colours are not right – they clash and the whole canvas is not portraying the true scene – it is better to put it on one side and start again.

I did not say discard it. It may be useful to use for comparison. At least he or she knew how to use the paint and brushes, but the result was just confusing.

So with your beliefs. You *know* deep within that you are more than just a body of flesh and bone. You find you have a capacity for deep thought and you have known from childhood that you have a conscience because you know right from wrong.

It is when you start to paint your picture that you encounter difficulties. There is too much space or not enough space; you are not sure exactly where those buildings were. You think they were right by the river; a friend tells you he remembers clearly they were some way from it. The first time you saw that scene there were autumnal colours, yet last week it was Spring and all the colours were different. But the scene was mainly the same. There was light and shade, but the people were dressed differently because of the weather. Perhaps they were the same people you saw earlier, but they appeared older.

Where is this analogy getting you? It is telling you there are different aspects of the same scene, a scene which is fundamentally the same.

I tell you, you are all My children. At heart, and I mean at heart, you are identical. You have equal capacity to love, to live, to care. But it is in the way you were brought up and the experiences you had that made you seem different. You were taught different rules about right and wrong and you looked on at different scenes which affected you deeply. Sometimes, when you queried situations or asked questions the answers you were given did not satisfy you. Then you could use your free will and decide whether you would just accept what you were told or try to find out more for yourselves.

And so, as the story became longer and more complicated, you decided which way you would go.

I was always with you and I sent others into your lives to guide or to test you, not for My sake, but for yours because I love you and want only what is best for you. But because I gave you free choice I have to let you find your own way.

When we talked about the ego recently, I said you all like to be right. There is only right, but you will not admit you have got a lot of it wrong – hence you argue where *discussion* would get you further. Not satisfied with arguing amongst yourselves in small groups, you take these thoughts much further until they become great issues. Then even when you bring in The Church, The Law, The United Nations, that you have set up to settle arguments, you still cannot agree.

Why?

Because there are closed minds, deaf ears, self-righteousness, lack of love and unselfishness, confusion, ignorance, revengefulness. Then I get blamed! So you ask "How much longer is it going to take?" You tell Me!

Misplaced Help

30.01.05

God, there must be millions of us today praying for peace in Iraq and for the safety of its people and the armed forces, there to help protect them. They so badly need their own government, a government that will allow them to live in peace and without fear. How much good is this prayer doing?

It is helping. You cannot stretch a square yard of cloth much further than its size; you cannot cause an ounce of gold to weigh more, even though you spread it out. In other words, while your prayers are helping because they can be stretched and spread out, there are many who are so self-destructive that they will stop at nothing. They cannot see ahead. They cannot bear the thought of being governed by others who will have different views, use different methods.

Should we, the British, and the Americans, be there? Our presence seems to cause more anger.

Sometimes you have to let people fight their own battles. You are not trying to protect them from another nation; you are trying to protect them

115

from themselves. You could say you are adding fuel to a fire that would otherwise have eventually died down.

Does that mean we should never go to the rescue of others?

War is never right, neither is shooting, bombing, maiming, terrifying others. You all know this and we have talked about it often. You can always find excuses for fighting, but you do not look for the peaceful solutions. Example is paramount at all times, in all situations.

But aren't all the Countries who are living in peace an example?

How many Countries are living in true peace and how many Countries are without weapons and armies and Ministers of War? You are afraid to live in real peace, giving up your weapons of destruction. You recall I said that when Countries demand peace and are brave enough to give up their weapons to prove their point, others will look on flabbergasted.

Should we let unlimited immigrants enter our small island?

There would be no requirement for unlimited immigrants if all countries were living in peace. There will always be those who wish to travel, to work elsewhere, but not from necessity because of fear and retribution. Go back to remembering you are each born on to your own space. Many are quite satisfied with their space and, if left to their own devices, would be happy to remain 'put', but it is the behaviour of others that usually makes them wish to, or have to, move. It all comes back to selfishness and not being satisfied with your plot.

Is a man living in one room in a crowded city better off than a native living in an isolated village under a tropical sun, with fruit and cereal available with very little effort? To each his own.

There will be those who say the one has no access to medical care, but that one may not require nor need it as much as the one living in a polluted town amidst squalor and shortage. And there are many forms of healing!

Comparison does not work.

Comparison amongst your religions causes big trouble. Why is a Jew more 'right' than a Muslim? Why is a Roman Catholic more 'right' than a Baptist?

They are none of them all right and none of them all wrong. Read Neale Donald Walsch's "The New Revelations" and "Tomorrow's God". Start your own little group of people to talk about what you believe. Promise beforehand that you will not argue, but that it will be an open-minded, loving discussion.

Start from the premise that I, God, am not a person, but pure Good. That I want nothing *from* you. Acknowledge that you will need to give up some of your preconceived beliefs. And if you do quote from your own particular Holy Book, be prepared to find contradictions in it, for I tell you man has added much that *I* disagree with!

Kindness

Dear God, I really believe that the death toll during the Iraq voting yesterday was less than feared because of a tremendous amount of prayer. You are always telling us we do not realise how powerful prayer is; surely there is proof here?

You still have a niggling feeling that you might be kidding yourself, yet if you did not believe in prayer why would you be so adamant about using it?

You think long before removing anyone from your daily healing list, knowing *I* can help a situation where you have no power on your own. I wish, my children, you could have seen the Light over Iraq and the way it helped the voters to overcome their fear as well as deterring many of the would-be terrorists.

Take heart. Use your power for Good on all possible occasions. It can do ONLY GOOD and eats up the Fear that has no real power. You all become so much stronger when you give up fear for the little 'nothing' that it is.

Why do we have so many fears, from the ridiculous like being afraid of mice or spiders, to the big as in fear of annihilation?

Right from babyhood you see examples of fear, portrayed by your parents and siblings, then from others as you grow. Then having hurt yourself, you begin to fear pain. Then you fear being parted from those you love and who look after you. Fear is contagious.

Now realise that you also pick up bravery. You admire heroes and heroic acts. You marvel at the stamina and determination around you. As you develop you need to be told of your own achievements and your own bravery. This is where parents and teachers can do so much to encourage all that is good and noble in the human soul.

One of the cruellest things is to 'put someone down', to take away their esteem, to make them feel less than worthy. You need encouragement and praise, and only your ego lets it get out of hand.

This is summed up by saying, use Kindness whenever possible. A kind word, a kind deed, a kind thought, work wonders, especially from unexpected sources.

Using The Light

Dear God, please tell us again about daily letting the Light into our bodies so that we help not only ourselves, but all those around us and the Countries to which we send this Light.

Many of you do this by starting your days with gratitude for all your blessings. By being thankful for your home, your food and your warmth; then by thinking of your friends and remembering those you know who are unwell.

All this lets in the Light. It is like opening your curtains before you do any other job and the daylight streams in, sometimes full of sunshine.

Picture this Light, the Light that I told you is too bright for you to even see with your eyes; picture it entering every cell of your mortal body, from the crown of your head to the tips of your toes and the tips of your fingers. It is the best dose of medicine you can take. It seeps into every atom of your Being. Be still and know this is happening. Be conscious of it. However rushed you are you can spare those few seconds to think about this happening.

Then as you go about your day, whether it be manual work, mental work, caring for others, even on holiday, your whole Being is suffused with Me.

This means All Good is consciously in and around you and you will come to feel it, to recognise it, and, most importantly, to give it off to others. Your whole demeanour will alter, your voice will lift, your eyes will sparkle. You are manifesting being A Being of God.

You can now feel good about yourself and about others. You will have helped yourself to see positive instead of negative thoughts and ideas that are ever flowing around. You will be enabled to help others because you have helped yourself.

118

You have experienced comfort instead of anxiety, perhaps loneliness, often pain. Just as a baby or a puppy likes to be picked up and cuddled close to you, you have put yourself into my arms and felt my heartbeat and my love. You are now able to face situations that were bothering you. You can tackle a job that yesterday you thought was too much for you. You made an effort and, like love, strength has manifested itself through you because you made yourself an open channel for My Light.

It is so easy. First you remember, then you pause, then you Let in the Light. In other words you are one with me consciously, instead of just unconsciously. You are ever full of Light just as you are ever full of Love and ever full of LIFE. It is a good feeling. You know it when you try it, you just forget to do it regularly.

Getting Outside Ourselves

I watched a programme recently about the most primitive tribe I had ever seen, yet even they were endeavouring to raise themselves up to 'something'. They sucked certain leaves and drank a potion that sent them on a 'high' and made them dance to the spirits.

This makes me realise that every human has a desire to experience something outside themselves, as if by instinct they know this is not all. Where do they 'go' during these bouts?

They move from one dreamland to another, just as drug-takers everywhere feel this desire to get outside themselves.

Yes, it is inborn in humanity to move on. To 'reach for the stars'. Also, in more advanced, less primitive beings, they want to 'get there faster'. They like the feeling of other-worldliness which occurs with drugs and alcohol. The fact that it is not the Truth that they experience does not matter to them. They can kid themselves that they like it.

Then what about atheists, who believe there is nothing else?

They wish to shut out the light instead of letting it in. They get their satisfaction by letting their ego make them feel slightly above the 'believers'. They kid themselves in the opposite direction. It matters not. They have the same free choice as you do.

I met a charming atheist recently and she stated she just didn't want anyone to try to alter her views. And I said, "Good for you. You are entitled to believe what you wish, though I myself cannot feel that way." I would like to have had more time to talk to her.

She wishes to stay in her own furrow. She feels safe there. If her life goes smoothly she is likely to remain with those thoughts. However, there might come a situation of great fear or loss or tragedy that could cause her to wonder and wish something different. Then she will wake up on earth instead of waiting until she arrives over here – on this higher plane.

That makes me think how difficult it is going to remain to alter the views of the different religions. They are content with what they believe, but unfortunately they all want us to believe their way. All that you tell us in these writings is to 'live and let live', yet try to sort out the Truth in each Teaching. Oh, God, we are so far from being One. That is when I feel 'flat' and 'useless'.

None of you is ever alone; not one of you. This is where you can all 'play your part' with your prayers for Peace and Oneness to manifest.

But all the Muslims and the Jews and the Christians are praying for us to believe their way. It becomes a war of prayers instead of a war of countries.

There are only wars through my people wanting their own way. When you pray for Peace you are praying for people to see Good, to alter their outlook, to be unselfish, to stop fearing. Try picturing them taking off their blinkers, see them looking upwards, see them joining hands with all people. Make a reality of these things and I tell you they will come to fruition. Look for the Good, know it HAS happened, then see it taking place, then do the praying. Remember that order. See the finished article, then see it being formed, then think about its blueprint. See the Great Hall of Learning, then think about where it will be built, then draw up the plans in detail.

Work is what you make it. It is either hard or worthwhile and enjoyable. The end product is either in your mind, being created, being considered, or it is such a long way off that you lose sight of the finished article. It is not hard work to pray, it is not tiring, it can be done anywhere under any conditions, and THERE IS AN END RESULT.

Dare to Demand

Oh, I dare to be hopeful. I dare to see this book in its finished form. It is 'out there' reaching all those who are seeking Truth. I am seeing 'the finished article'; I have made a reality of it; then I watched it being handled, printed, bound; now I am continuing with its content. God, I have 'thought' it the way you keep telling us.

"See it manifesting," you say, "then work it out." I have done that and I feel elated.

Good, my child. You are learning. Again I say, we do not waste our resources. All will come to pass and in your heart you have always known it would.

All of you, keep on keeping on. Pray with your thoughts for Peace and Good and Plenty for all my children on the earth plane. It is there, but it requires distributing equally. You can experience absolute joy in Peace and Good and Plenty for it is what you all need, what I mean you to have.

It is man who has interfered with the distribution, thinking he knows better how to live, how to try to make others live, how to feed and how to make others sell their food to make him rich. Is there yet unselfishness in every business transaction? Is there absolute Truth in man's every action, every motive?

Wouldn't it be good to start up Universities to teach Absolute Truth and Transparency and Unselfishness!

You, each one of you, can start up that in your heart centres. You do not need to pay nor to study to do that work. Place the honest, caring people at the head of every trade, every organisation, be it Church, Government, Health Service, School, Business Company, Construction of all kinds.

How wonderful that would be. There would be no ill-practice, no lies, no cover-ups, only everyone working for the good of others.

What is stopping you?

Alas, greed and selfishness. It is time we demanded Honesty in all places.

Thought

Dear God, I long to finish this second book, yet I shall feel lost when it is completed. What of my future?

All is NOW, remember?

Yes, of course, but I do get weary. Not weary of this work – that could never happen – but tired in body.

All living things, be it birds, flowers, trees or humans, take a rest.

121

Do we need to rest in the heaven world – on the next plane?

You will not keep on endlessly at the same 'job'; you will change your 'tasks', but they will not seem like the work you do now. You will be working with love and joy, free from all pain and weariness. You will be working with Mind not with body. Movement will be without effort, instantaneous. Your thinking will be instantaneous. So many other souls will be working with you and much more planning will have been done and thought given by those who have gone before.

Consider now how much of what you do has already been planned beforehand. You purchase ready-made articles from clothes to cutlery, from ready-grown vegetables to ready-built houses.

Here you can be in at the conception or in at the 'kill'. You can do that on the earth plane also according to the item and your place of origin.

There will be so much we do not need on our next wavelength.

The clutter will cease, but the need to progress will continue and the need to impress upon your earth plane fresh ideas. Just as you are letting in my words now, so others are letting in my guidance with plant propagation, engine design, land maintenance, animal breeding, baby rearing.

I do not think of engineering as being something spiritual!

Why not?

It is too material and I am sure there will not be machines in heaven! Nor things like spoons and forks come to think of it.

You would not take a refrigerator to the North Pole nor ice skates to the Sahara, but they have their uses in the right places.

So we are not wrong to make planes and cars and run underground trains?

You enjoy using ingenuity – there is nothing wrong with that. You use imagination – there is nothing wrong with that. Then you stray from the useful to the useless. You make guns and other weapons.

But you have said we need help from above to create, so who sows the seeds of weapon-design into our mortal minds?

Do you think *I* sow seeds of murderous thoughts into your minds?

Well, we have to use our Thought to make weapons and commit murder.

Should you not have used a small 't' for that kind of thought? There is the little mortal mind, and the Higher Mind which uses Thought, with a capital

T, at all times. Real Thought is Good Thought, God Thought, Loving Thought. That kind of Thought THINKS FIRST.

So why did we make guns and bombs? Just because we didn't think first?

You know the answer. It is because you think you want what is not yours and because you think you haven't **enough** of what you have!

But there are thousands of people who really haven't enough of what they **need***?*

And you know why that is!

Yes, because we are selfish, thoughtless and do not share. And because we have invaded other countries and made them think they need the kinds of things we need, or think we need. It is the same old story which has been continuing for centuries.

You would do well to remember the saying, "Live and Let Live". Think deeply about that saying. Doesn't it cover a multitude of what you do!

Yes. I have never thought about that saying really deeply.

Me, Betty, Speaking

I find myself running out of questions. The more I read and re-read what has been conveyed to me, I realise we are in control of our own lives and the outcome of our actions is up to us.

God keeps reminding us that we have Free Will, Free Choice. Individually we need to ask for guidance, but only if we wish to use it and not just go our own way.

We need to 'Wake Up' to so much simple Truth.

This could be a perfect world now; in fact it is, but we keep messing it up, trying to alter it, trying to make others think as we do. The trouble is, those who are selfish and domineering 'take over' and we let them. So it is again a case of putting the unsuitable people in positions of power.

I have a friend who follows a certain cult and she does not wish to discuss this work with me in case we fall out! How is that for keeping on your blinkers? We could agree to differ in a civilised way. I would love to have discussions with nuns, monks, priests, Muslims and others. I already have wonderful discussions with a Jew and he realises he has become a seeker after real Truth and finds much help and satisfaction in reading what I am being told, along with other writings.

I suppose one difficulty is, there are those who think this work of mine is just that. Mine. But it is so obvious that it is not. The Truth sticks out a mile, in fact to infinity. How can you deny its simple yet profound Truth?

When I pick up other books that I inwardly know are the Truth, I find the same messages in them, just put in a slightly different way. These books include those of Neale Donald Walsch and White Eagle. All are telling us how to live in harmony. All are decrying war.

There is SO MUCH that God didn't say. Some statements are laughable, pathetic, gross. They make no sense, but man thought he was proclaiming a truth. Trouble was he didn't go deep into his heart centre to find the real Truth.

On the whole we are thoughtless. Or we act then think. Or we blame others instead of ourselves. The little ego still loves to get its own way.

If you doubt your instinct, read about those elephants and other animals that left the site prior to the tsunami. They used their instinct. Then those wonderful elephants went back to help and are now using their strength to move great loads of debris. I am going to read about that again and again. What an example.

What are YOU looking for? Do your doctrines meet all your queries? Do you follow rules and regulations because you *feel* they are right or because you have been told to. If the latter, do you pause to consider their sense? Do you still think it matters what you wear? Do you still think death is *the end*? Do you still feel a need to wear black to a funeral? Why? Of course you are sorry for the mourners, but does it help them to be surrounded by black?

As death is so wonderful for the one who has gone on, why not have an enlightening celebration for their release from this particular world? Of course those who are still here are sad; unbelievably sad. But who for? They are sad for themselves and all who are affected by the physical loss of one they loved. *They* need your understanding, your compassion and your spiritual strength. *You* need to be able to give them that.

How can we help each other if we are unable to put ourselves in their position, be it through loss, failed business, family trauma, homelessness, and all the hundreds of other things that affect every one of us?

Even the weather affects many of us.

All these things are an opportunity for us to use our Thought, to turn all that is negative into positive. What a lot of rubbish goes through our minds on a daily basis!

Good, positive thought creates good, positive vibes. These are picked up by others and multiplied. All through this writing I have been privileged to do, the Power of Prayer has dominated. Prayer isn't getting down on your knees, it is proclaiming the Truth in your Mind at all times. Turning all negative thoughts into positive ones.

We do need to spend quiet periods thinking of all those in need and sending them the Light, holding them in the Light. This is the Light of Good, God. It is so powerful and effective. Use it not only for those you love, but particularly over those Countries at war and over the starving. Also over world leaders that they may work for the good of all. Also include the Press, Television and Radio, for the media has great power and with our help can convey Truth rather than sensationalism and innuendos.

We need to discipline ourselves. That can sound an unpleasant word, something we don't wish to do, but look what a mess every town is in, let alone the whole world, through lack of discipline.

Would we have drunks and bullies and thieves and even murderers if we had been brought up to use discipline? Now this is where we can look back and see how Convents and Monasteries worked. But do they work for everyone? No of course not. Most of us would be bored, useless and distracted by that life. It is easier to be 'good' in those circumstances because you shut yourself away from the outside world, away from temptation, away from the distractions of modern life. But were we meant to live like that?

How do we learn without experience? How do we help others financially and materially and physically while we are 'inside'? I am sure it is fine for the few and I know their prayers help tremendously when they are for the good of mankind. But we are all ONE and need to intermix, to laugh, to play, to cry together.

Just realise how one day, there will be peace on earth. We shall walk and talk without fear. We shall live for each other, be there for each other, help each other for no reward except the pleasure of giving of ourselves. Keeping up with the Jones's will be a thing of the past.

And all this is in our hands. Actually it is in our Minds, but we need to put it into practice. I hope I reincarnate back here when this has manifested!

Old Age

God, old age can seem really ugly. I know of several cases at this moment in time – one famous, the others just ordinary people. I have asked before, why do we try to make them live on beyond their healthy state?

Firstly, there are no 'ordinary' people nor famous people. All are equal, all are as important as one another and it is you who put them up or down.

Yes, I know what you are saying, but I mean some are known worldwide for what they do or have achieved.

Secondly, you have a natural instinct to save life, but you can take this too far, you can turn this into a desired achievement or you do it because you forget, or do not believe, that another life awaits every one of you.

So really the medical profession causes unnecessary time to be spent on this earth plane, holding us back from natural progression?

You can put it that way. But I have told you, you 'die' when you are meant to 'die', just as you are born when you are meant to be born. And you are meant to be 'born' back on to a higher plane at a specific time. You could say, there are no miscarriages in either direction.

This sounds dangerous ground. It appears to make suicide and murder OK.

It makes them not an accident. The one who is killed has moved on.

But what of the murderer?

They either get killed also, as in battle – which is murder – or they spend time locked up with only their conscience for company.

God, why do I not feel properly tuned-in to You?

Because something you feel to be complex is now sounding too simple. If you all lived as you were 'designed' to live, your lives would be simple, without stress, without anxiety, without sorrow, without rush, without shortage.

126

But what about the natural anxiety we feel for those we love or those we lose or those without life's necessities?

To start with, anxiety isn't *natural*. Those you love are always in My Care and those you 'lose' are not lost *anywhere*, they are just no longer on your 'wavelength', within your line of vision. As for those without life's necessities, you know they could be better off with more care from those who have more than enough. We come back to unselfishness and caring.

And old age!

Do you envisage ageing on the next plane?

No, because we shall have overcome death and see it as a means of progressing.

Whereas now you believe in death and deterioration. You *expect* to age. You are brought up to anticipate wrinkles and inactivity and incapability. You think you 'wear out'. Recall a great friend of yours who looked thirty years younger than her age at death – you believe she looked as she did because of what she believed and put into practice. You are right to believe that. Your Mind is your teacher.

But what of animals – they do not appear to age as we do, they just look a bit older.

They do not *think* about wrinkles and rheumatics; they do not expect to age; they just take each day as it comes.

Your thoughts, your outlook, your expectations, your determination, all these things affect your physical bodies. Expect trouble and you draw it to you like a magnet. Expect Good at every turn and all dark places become light. Open yourselves at all times to being positive.

Some people are afraid to travel alone, they allow themselves to anticipate trouble, thereby sowing seeds of doubt and unease, then they wonder why 'everything happens to me', meaning the negative things.

Others know they are and will be safe at all times – in other words never alone. They see the flowers before the buds open. They do not say 'the sun has gone in', instead they know it is just some clouds that are hiding the eternal sun. They have conditioned themselves to remember the sun never 'goes in'.

Do some people choose to linger on after their 'sell by date'?

Some of my people try to cling on to their earth life because they fear there is nothing else. They may have said they have no desire to live, but towards the end of their earthly days they wonder. Could there perhaps be another life? It is then that fear loses its grip and gives way to hope, then hope becomes a reality – the reality of Life without end. You Wake Up in the twinkling of an eye; it is less effort than taking one step, just one step.

The Same Truth

I am amazed when I re-read Neale Donald Walsch's writings to find how similar God's statements are to him and to me. Then I realise it is all the same Truth, just put in a slightly different way. Yet it is all simple and interchangeable.

Neale and I ask different questions or we ask similar questions in our own way.

I find this very comforting. We are both asking questions that all of us must think about in our minds or, more correctly, in our Minds. And isn't the Truth simple?

There are no frills, no 'wrapped up' answers, no continual references to Holy Books or what God has said in the past. In fact, God keeps telling us so much about what He didn't say in the past.

And though we now know God isn't a person, but pure Good, we still talk to 'Him'.

At this moment, I can only liken this to listening to Strauss being played in Vienna where it originated to hearing that glorious, uplifting, happy music being played in Australia or England. It doesn't change. Excuse me God for bringing You down to the level of Strauss, but You must have infused him with that wonderful gift!

It is good to note the clergy of most denominations are endeavouring to see each other's points of view. And interesting to see on our television screens that we were asked to vote on a new set of ten commandments. How they have changed and how their position has changed on the list! Apparently the First is now 'Treat others as you would wish to be treated'.

Now we need, so badly, a new form of energy to be discovered. We cannot restore all the damage we have done, but we could cease to use up the diminishing oil. God, please cause Minds to open to 'pick up' this awaiting knowledge.

Treats

What has happened to Treats? When I was a child a treat was riding in a car, going on a picnic, a seaside holiday, cream, just very occasionally being allowed to stay up until about 9 o'clock, going to a party, having a party dress. Oh, and being taken to a London Pantomime.

All those things are now part of everyday life. Children are stuffed with all the wrong food, fizzy drinks, sweets ad lib, continuous television, and trips abroad are commonplace.

As they become teenagers their 'treats' appear to be drug-taking and binge-drinking. I know there are exceptions, but I am talking about the seeming majority. Where are we going God?

You are marking time.

But you say there is no Time.

Exactly! You cannot waste Time because it is eternal. There is progress, but some choose not to progress. There is regression and some choose that.

I blame parents. They neither set a good example nor use discipline.

They have free choice!

But at what cost to children?

You have heard of the Indigo Children. They are far beyond your earth years and are returning to bring reason out of chaos. The tribes you were thinking about earlier are better parents, as are animals. They teach discipline and example. They often go without themselves to succour their young, but they do not 'spoil' them. Their offspring are taught by example and love – yes love, unselfish love.

The Western World has far more than it needs, yet it wants more and more. More money, more leisure, more entertainment, more of what is thought to be desirable. Many have lost the joy of loving and giving, especially in simple ways.

What is going to happen?

Too much seeming comfort is causing discomfort. Conscientiousness is sprouting in many directions, altering people's ideas. There is a move towards compassion and common sense.

Your television screens could be great teachers. They could be your best means of altering outlook. World News is necessary, but portrayal of war, murder, violence and foul language just for entertainment's sake is cause for concern. You, all of you, who desire a better environment, have the power to make your feelings known. You have become complacent. You do not have to accept the unacceptable. People Power without violence can be very effective. It is in your hands.

What is Faith?

God, I have been asked "What is faith?"

Faith is something you are taught or something you acquire. You put your faith into something or someone. Often it helps you to do that – it becomes a prop.

But isn't faith very important? It is what people believe, practise, honour, admit.

What is belief? That is something you use. You can have faith in your car; you can believe it will get you from a to z, and usually it does. But if there is a serious fault in the engine it will break down.

You cannot believe all you are told. You cannot believe all you read. But you *can* be faithful to what you know is Truth. Faith and Belief can let you down, but Truth never can.

You talk about different Faiths, different Beliefs. There is Truth in all of them for they are forms of religion, but look how religion has changed over the centuries.

You watch documentaries about different tribes, some of whom still haven't seen white men. They have their beliefs, their faith, their form of religion. All humans are looking for a higher understanding and their very act of looking carries them onward. You all have an innate Knowing and a wishing to progress.

These tribes you speak of are less evolved spiritually, yet often more evolved materially – they do not decimate the earth as you do. You imagine becoming more evolved on the next plane and, just as these tribes can become more evolved on the earth plane, so you can evolve on different planets, far, far beyond anything you can conceive of in your present state.

I would ask you to query your faith and your beliefs. By seeking and reading you often change your beliefs. Take your progress at a speed that is comfortable to you. Do not try to rush things. Be open to change, to altering your little mind by listening to your Higher Mind.

130

Sit on the wall and meditate before jumping off. If you are in a perfect situation it may not matter which side you land, for you will still progress. However, there is usually a better side, not necessarily because it is more beautiful, but because you can do more good in the shadow or the thicket. It is while you are on the wall that you need to ask for guidance, strength and love to accompany you on your journey.

Some choose the easy way, some the difficult. Some use blind faith, some use an inner knowing.

Getting it All Wrong

1.4.05

There is so much tragedy through this second earthquake, so many thousands suffering in Africa, endless unrest and terrorism all over the world; God where is hope and happiness?

It is there, but it is harder to see than in the past for news travels much faster and in pictures as well as words. Pictures make more impact.

You are shown the horror, the fighting, the starvation, the unrest – that is News. How many of your television channels make a point of displaying Peace and Love and Beauty? They are there, but they are not sensational.

I have told you before, my children want what they do not need; in most cases speed, weed and greed. They have lost the joy of experiencing the simple things. Not only children, but adults too, can relish the sight of newborn lambs, animals playing, birds singing, wild flowers blooming *en masse*. These things are free for all to enjoy. And many do. It is the grasping, dissatisfied youth that appears to you to abound and then they grow to be dissatisfied and resentful adults.

We are back to discipline. You train your horses, your dogs, even your birds, but how many people train their children? We are speaking of the masses. The thousands that do care, do live happily, do not make the News.

I know all this is true, but who is going to teach this discipline? Parents seem to have lost their control; schools are becoming horrendous places and streets in towns at night are scaring the elderly.

Where is example? The tribes we speak of have more discipline, are satisfied with less, therefore not always wanting yet more and more. There is a vast difference between need and want, as you know. Recall how one of your sons spent his birthday playing with pieces of wood, a hammer and nails in preference to toys. A small child finds more comfort spending time with its parents than watching television. When parents give time and patience and impart knowledge, they create a bond that no artificial entertainment can do.

When these better orientated children later attend school they will be more willing to continue learning from teachers. They will have a desire to get somewhere with their lives.

All this is common sense, but where has common sense gone and how long is it going to take to regain it?

As I have said – example, discipline and patience, combined with love and understanding, are your tools. Use them. Use them on yourselves so that you can then use them on your children and on their children. The bullies and the tearaways are not happy. They just do not know what to do with themselves. They need leadership and education.

Does junk food affect people's behaviour?

Feed your plants with too much artificial food, too much fertiliser, insufficient water, too much heat, too much cold, and see what happens to *them*. Is it any wonder that human bodies manifest peculiarities, malnutrition, poor growth?

Again I feel it is a pity we have free will. We make such a mess of using it.

But how would you progress without it?

Patience

How difficult I find it to be patient – whether awaiting good news, sad news, disappointment, delays of all kinds, even sunny weather. What is the best way to deal with this?

If you will remember that you are always in My care, that your every need is known, you will find it easier to be patient. Impatience is a form of worry, fear, mistrust.

Know, know, that all things work together for good for those who love God. You have free will to rush ahead, alter plans, force an issue, then when things go wrong you know you have only yourself to blame. Wait patiently and all will work out in a gentler way. This does not mean that you just sit back and do nothing.

Pray, think, consider. Absorb the love that is being poured down upon you, all of you. We do not neglect you. We know your every need, your every desire. We know what is truly in your hearts. We know even better than you do for you are inclined to half-listen.

You cannot see ahead as we can. Remember the ant. It cannot see as far as the rockery or the pond – all that is a long way off – but to you looking on, you can see clearly and you can see any pitfalls.

Time to you seems real and it can so easily seem long or short according to what you are doing, whether you are enjoying yourselves or whether you are stressed and working 'against time'. All is Now. Make the most of each minute because once it has gone you cannot go back and re-live it, except in memory. And it is when you use memory that you realise how you endured much that was dreary, worrying to you, and seemed endless. Now in retrospect you recall even a few years in a flash. You came through. You can see whether you moved wisely through that period, being patient, or whether you rushed ahead willy-nilly.

We KNOW your wishes, your aspirations, your desires.

Do You direct others so that our best interests are met?

Have you never felt directed? Recall certain things you have done, sometimes on 'the spur of the moment' as you say. Recall how you feel a nudge that makes you say "that wasn't me". Of course we direct all our children all the time, but whether they respond is up to them. We direct, even give a gentle push at times, but we never demand or command or compel.

Those of you who know you are on a good path, know how to act, how to listen, how to sort out your thoughts.

Pray for Patience. It is already yours, my child.

Seeing Religion from the Other Side

God, because of Pope John Paul's recent passing over, it has suddenly struck me – what happens to the different religions in the next world? When we find we are All One and that there is only One Truth there will be no need to feel a Quaker or a Muslim or a Catholic.

Firstly, you will not 'arrive' in a mitre or a turban or a crown. You will find yourself attired in what I will call a raiment. This is a simple flowing garment and all others will look alike. There is no hierarchy, no rank.

You may become aware that some raiments are brighter than others; they will emanate more light; they will attract more attention, not because of position, but because of spiritual attraction.

Liken this to wattage in your electric light bulbs, some are as low as 5 watts, some are 500 watts, but whereas these are used to see better, the light on this plane exudes from your soul according to how much you have developed it previously.

But that doesn't mean a Rabbi or an Archbishop will automatically show a brighter light than a gypsy, does it?

Oh no. The light will show the real, the true progress of the soul spiritually. An enlightened gypsy could show more light than a misinformed preacher. You know by now that there is Truth in many places. You also know that there is positive corruption and malpractice in some 'high places'. Gold and silver, spires and domes can mean little; a rose or a teardrop can be more magnificent than a mountain.

It must be a great shock for those who have felt so 'right' when on earth, to find themselves of little consequence and unnoticed.

But do not forget that every soul has the gift and the ability to become one of the brightest lights. So much you have held dear will drop away quite easily when it is put in perspective. You will desire to progress but not to become 'top dog'. You, yourself, love mongrels more than pedigree dogs. Why? Because you have found their intelligence and their loyalty and love. On the earth plane it is you, the humans, who decide why a dog should become top of its breed. Does it mean it has the best character, more loyalty, more love? No, you judge by appearances! Here we do not judge, but we know what qualities to look for. We know what work, what thought, what endeavour, what dedication has gone before.

You are all equal, but some of you have hidden or forgotten to use your beautiful attributes. Over here, where all is Love, it is easier to bring forth all that is beautiful and true and admirable. You will not judge, you will not wish to argue, instead you will look on with awe, understanding, amazement.

You will find you are drawn to those who will be able to help you most. You will also be drawn to those who need *your* help. You will not only be happy, you will be busy, very busy, and fulfilled in a way you never felt before on your earth plane.

Oh, how I look forward to this experience.

Karma

I don't think I have the right conception of karma. I believed it was a 'putting right of' things we had done wrong in a past life'. Please explain God.

Karma is opportunity. You hear people say, "Oh, it is his karma", meaning he has 'brought it on himself'. Those people do not realise that soul has asked for its opportunities, its experiences. These can be difficult experiences; occurrences that were not satisfactorily dealt with in a previous life, or they can be beautiful experiences. You are given some obstacles, some problems, some glorious opportunities – all in order that you may progress.

You have free choice as to how you deal with these situations when they arise. Your life, your progress, is in your hands. Your innate knowing tells you how to act, but you do not always act in accordance with your knowing. This can cause delay in your progress or you can move ahead ready for your next hurdle.

But what about those of us who have done really wrong deeds in a past life – doesn't it matter how long we take to put things right?

There is No Time. There IS progress. When you 'get things wrong' you are really harming yourself more than the other person. You cannot take a Life, for Life is eternal. But you can cause your conscience to bother you deeply. You can put off trying to right that wrong, but your conscience does not forget, even though in your present life it may not remember what went wrong in the past, you can listen to that innate feeling as to how you deal with a situation that crops up now.

You can improve your life conditions during every moment of your day and you do this, through many, many incarnations, until you find a 'Peace which passes all understanding'. Then you are truly ready to move on.

How does the 'injured party' learn from this?

How they deal with their seeming injustice or injury or hurt is a lesson for them. Their understanding can grow; their compassion one for another can be manifested. Their 'trials and tribulations' can teach them also how to progress.

So does all wrong eventually become righted?

Yes, because I have told you there really is no right and wrong. All is perfect, but your thinking and your actions cause problems that were not there.

So this is where forgiveness is so important.

Forgiveness is all important. Forgiving others is an act of kindness, but forgiving yourself is imperative to your own progress – and your peace of mind.

Hope

My beautiful 'Peace' rose is looking me straight in the eyes and asking, "What do you wish to know?" And I feel empty of questions; I wonder why. There is only one thing on my mind that really matters and that is 'When am I going to get this present work published? What further steps can I take to achieve this?'

And every time you open one of your 'guide books' you are told those in the spirit world know your every thought, your every need, your every feeling. They are there to help and guide you. This comforts you, but only temporarily. Doubt and fear and disappointment soon take over your thoughts again. You trust, but you lack patience. You persevere, but you 'droop'. You feel guilty when you don't do this work, yet tired when you do. Why do you think you still 'hear' Me, even though sometimes you doubt if you will?

Because I know without a doubt that I am privileged to be a 'channel for your light' and that this work will go on and on through hundreds of us who are trying to help and awaken others to their journey and purpose in this life. I know it is likely to be a very long time, in our sense of time, before great numbers of people think this way – before they realise this simple way of living in peace and happiness.

Never, never give up hope. There is growth. Once again you are seeing growth in your garden at this time, but how long has it taken you to really, truly notice the growth of nature? For most of your life you took it for granted; now you purposefully look for it and at it and marvel at it. So it is with this Truth you write about. It has always been there, but how many truly notice it?

Human Beings take much longer to come to maturity than a shrub or a flower. Animals and plant life mature with very little help compared with a baby. Babies need much help and encouragement from their parents, especially in the art of feeding and developing their talents and learning about certain dangers.

136

Here we come to the present loss of example, thought and care that is being given by young parents to their children. I have said before, discipline and love are the first lessons. Now, having learned the hard way, parents are finding the results of wrong feeding. It is going to take time to put 'right' all the 'wrong' that has been caused by taking short cuts, evading thought and care, with the resultant catastrophes.

Do you think you have your priorities in the correct order?

Personally, I think they are horrendously wrong. Oh, I see where I am going! They, the modern parents, are not prepared to wait for what they want. They put the owning of a house and cars and entertainment before the needs of their children. Both parents usually work to bring in enough income to enable them to have what they could do without until after giving more time and care to bringing up their children. They are not setting the right example. There is nothing demeaning about a mother staying at home to nurture and start educating her offspring.

I am certain correct food and drink will bring a return of non-belligerent children in the home and consequently when at school. It is unnatural for children to be so full of hate and resistance to learning. Are we at last getting back on to the right track?

Yes, and it will seem a slow progression because the root cause of the trouble has not happened overnight. Attitudes alter slowly, both in parents and children, but a beginning has been made. Respect for all ages and all professions has to return. Thought for others in all things has to be exercised. Thought in Government, thought in Teaching the young, thought in educating the older children, thought in questioning all ways of living, eating, travelling, co-operating, living as equal Beings.

Your every act has an effect, not only on yourselves, but on others. Every thought affects your way of living and the lives of those around you, and, incidentally, in the whole world. That is why prayer is so effective. True, unselfish prayer benefits all my people all over the earth.

When a catastrophe occurs it brings out so much good, so much unselfishness that it is seen, literally seen, but prayer performs that Good in a quieter way, in a subtle way, and it is absorbed and it spreads. Pray for all that is good, all that is beneficial to All peoples, all that will help you to live in peace one with another.

And, yes, keep on with this work. Those sentences you read are not meaningless!

The Strength of the Light

My golden rose has its head turned fully upwards to the sunshine. It is absorbing its rays and is truly a picture of Peace. What is it telling me?

It is telling you too to be at peace; at peace with yourself and with all that surrounds you. Keep knowing, all of you, that the things that concern you are being taken care of by wiser, more evolved beings than yourselves.

You have prayed for help and protection and guidance for those on your list and you pray for their protection from accident and false moves. Those pure, unselfish thoughts cause a beautiful light to go forth from you to the 'workers', (angels as some of you think of them); then that light is poured forth to those people and countries that need that help and guidance. It puts them also in tune with all that is good and beautiful and helpful. You include surgeons and nurses and carers in that light that they may be guided to do what is best for their fellow humans.

The workers on this higher plane know how to use the light that you ask for, just as you know who to hold in it. Think of the six pointed star of light. The light goes up from you and your patient or subject on whom you are using it, then it is sent back revivified and strengthened to your subject and to you. Thus the two triangles merge, making that beautiful star of light.

Those of you who send forth the light need light sent back to you to strengthen you in your endeavours and to help you to Keep On Keeping On. You, yourself, learned all this in your White Eagle work. You are causing channels to work upwards and then downwards to complete the Whole.

The light is always there – you are causing it to be more consciously used, more 'felt'.

Those of you who have experienced an electric shock know the unseen power of that element. Believe Me, when I say that is as nothing compared with the Power of the Light you are using. It is mighty, nothing gets in its way; nothing interrupts it. And according to the openness of the receiver of the Light, so it manifests accordingly.

If you could see and better understand this process you would be using it at all times, in all circumstances. It overcomes all seeming evil, all illness, all fear. Although you forget it much of the time, you cannot get away from it. It is a continuous sending and receiving, an eternal process; Good in action at all times. Use it more my dear ones.

Behaviour

Why is it taking so long for Good to overcome seeming evil? Why are people using ugly language, aggressive behaviour? What has happened to beautiful clothes and melodious music? Where are the wonderful voices of trained singers?

I ask you, what has happened to discipline? Where is example? Where is gentleness? Who decides what you shall watch on your most powerful tool, namely television screens? Who decides who are 'stars' in their field?

When enough of you dare to demand higher standards, higher standards in all things from behaviour to food, to entertainment, to equal distribution of global food, fairer living conditions, the situation will begin to improve.

None of you should feel helpless in bringing forth these improvements. You have means of making your wishes known without being belligerent. Quiet, persuasive action is more effective than ranting and raving.

Remember "The man who pays the piper names the tune".

You, yourself, are horrified at the amount of waste that goes on, from food to overindulgence of gifts to children. Teach children to appreciate their home, their food and their pleasures. It would mean far more for them to have more of their parents' time and attention than a whole box of toys.

Adults surrounded by all they could wish for often long for companionship and meaningful conversation. Notice how good you feel when you help others, when you give of your time, your love, your thought. Also notice how good you feel when you receive the love and thought of others. You were born to be intermingling yet individual beings.

I am sure that television could be a wonderful means of raising our standards, then I remember how the internet is now interfering with moral standards, even enabling our children to get involved with pornography and paedophiles. There seems no end to the length some people will go to drag us down to a level lower than reptiles.

Do not demean reptiles!

Sorry!

You, all of you, have free choice in all things. How you use it is up to you. And that Star of Light we were talking about earlier today can be used for Good in all matters, including matter!

Epilogue

Dear God, I feel the time has come for me to end this present dialogue with you, at least in this second book-form. Will you give me an Epilogue please.

Your golden rose has closed its petals. It has not died; it has become a bud and is lying beside the earlier pink rose, as if they are taking a rest.

Those of you who have read this book to the end have absorbed more than you may think.

Some of you 'lap it up', thirsty for its Truth; others who have been deeply indoctrinated by other teachings, have a few queries in your minds.

If you were not seeking the Truth you would not be reading this and similar books.

This book is written by a simple soul who found she did not want to argue with My words. In fact, she made a rule never to alter one word of what she 'heard'. That is why she is used. She has intelligence, as have you all, but she was not deeply rooted in any one faith.

Read with your heart and Higher Mind and you will find what your Soul Seeks – namely Peace, Love and Contentment. You will come to realise that Life is eternal. You do not fall into a prolonged sleep, as the rosebuds appear to have done, but at your seeming death you will find yourself instantly in another dimension. And I, God, Good, Love, am always with you.

All blessings are yours, there for you to use at all times.

AMEN

Recommended Further Reading

Author	Title	Publisher
Neale Donald Walsch	Conversations With God Trilogy & Others	Hodder & Stoughton
Marlo Morgan	Mutant Message Down Under	Thorsons
Annie Kirkwood	Mary's Message to the World	Piatkus
Louise L. Hay	You Can Heal Your Life & Others	Eden Grove Editions
Thom Hartmann	The Last Hours of Ancient Sunlight	Hodder & Stoughton
" "	The Prophet's Way	Mythical Books
White Eagle	Many Titles	White Eagle Publishing Trust

INDEX